Getting to the Heart of Leadership

Getting to the Heart of Leadership

Emotion and Educational Leadership

Megan Crawford

SAGE

Los Angeles • London • New Delhi • Singapore • Washington DC

MT

First published 2009

SAGE Publications Ltd
1 Oliver's Yard
55 City Road
London EC1Y 1SP

SAGE Publications Inc.
2455 Teller Road
Thousand Oaks, California 91320

SAGE Publications India Pvt Ltd
B 1/I 1 Mohan Cooperative Industrial Area
Mathura Road
New Delhi 110 044

SAGE Publications Asia-Pacific Pte Ltd
33 Pekin Street #02–01
Far East Square
Singapore 048763

Library of Congress Control Number: 2008927371

British Library Cataloguing in Publication data

A catalogue record for this book is available from the
British Library

ISBN 978-1-84787-169-5
ISBN 978-1-84787-170-1 (pbk)

Typeset by Dorwyn, Wells, Somerset
Printed in India at Replika Press Pvt Ltd
Printed on paper from sustainable resources

2/9/10

for Philip with much love

Contents

Acknowledgements

This book would not have happened without my own emotional coherence, both in the process of writing, in the research work I did, and in encouraging me to become involved in academic life. I would like to thank: Marianne Coleman, for all her help with the thinking; my colleagues at the Institute of Education, especially Peter Earley, Derek Glover and Louise Stoll for supporting the writing process; Ron Glatter, for getting me started and encouraging me to continue; and my family for their support.

I also want to thank Matthew Waters at Sage who has been so helpful throughout.

Finally, I would like to thank all the headteachers who shared their time, their lives and their thoughts on headship with me. Some are included in depth in this book, but without all of you this book would not have been written.

Chapter 1

An emotional journey

The unstoppable humming of the most universal of melodies that only dies down when we go to sleep.
(Damasio, *Looking for Spinoza*, 2004)

Introduction

This book is about people who become leaders in educational settings, and how understanding the emotional journey they make as leaders can help them progress in that journey. You may already be one of those leaders, or aspire to become one. I hope to make you more aware of the various debates around emotion and leadership, and inspire you to read more. As well as this, the book gives suggestions for reading if you wish to follow up particular areas for more personal understanding. The book draws on my own deep professional interest in how the headteacher's emotional geography (Hargreaves, 2000: 152) can profoundly influence the emotional climate of the school, which has been reflected in my earlier writings (Crawford, 2002; 2003; 2004). My personal background in counselling and psychology means that I am concerned with emotional reality and the construction of the self and, how headteachers, as people, function in leadership roles. How does personal emotional reality shape their view and practice of leadership? What influence does emotion have on the ways that educational leaders view and recall leadership situations? To begin to answer these questions, I

> will be stressing the interplay between leadership, emotion, and the organisation and how growing understandings of emotion can enhance and even challenge some of the prevailing orthodoxies in regard to educational leadership.

First, this book is both the story of emotion and leadership, and also the stories of individual headteachers told in order to help others reflect on their own journeys through leadership. I draw on research (conducted between summer 2004 and summer 2007) with 11 primary and secondary headteachers based on their own reflections on emotions as well as the influence of their life history, and school context. The concept of a 'personal leadership narrative' will be outlined to show not only that an individual's complexity is not adequately served by competency approaches to emotion, but also that school leadership, and in particular, headship is a complex synergy of emotion and leadership. As we go through, I will be sharing some of those examples so you as a leader can reflect on their similarities and differences. As a book, it is a journey both through and about the stories that people tell to each other and to themselves that shape the meaning of the work they do, and the leadership that they carry out.

Second, this book is being written at a time when the very sustainability of headship is being discussed, researched and debated at policy and personal levels. Some of the concepts, such as system leadership, federated leadership, and non-teacher leadership, have an emotional dimension that currently remains unexplored. This book will suggest what some of these might be, and how this could affect leadership practice in the future.

Layers of meaning in leadership

When researching in education, I have always adopted as a

basic principle that social reality is made up of many layers. These layers include the uniqueness of every person: their personality and life history, the place where they work, and the people they work with. The stance taken in this book is that these layers are woven together, and given their meaning, by the affective aspects of social reality. In education today, more than ever before, there is an emphasis on the importance of extending knowledge of the affective domain for practitioners. This is reflected in the field of educational leadership studies.

In the book, I'll explore literature about emotion that is not explicitly concerned with educational leadership, with the aim of stimulating your interest so you might want to go away and read more. I also seek to value the personal voice and life stories of educational leaders as a way of exploring leadership issues. My aim in writing is to refocus attention on the individuals who become leaders in schools and in particular those who choose headship. This is because their individuality is far less considered in the literature, although the nature of educational leadership is already well explored. In much of the current work on educational leadership, the contested nature of leadership stands out. This is reflected in the emphasis on multiple ways of describing and analysing it. This trend has been described by Leithwood as 'adjectival leadership', where the description somehow becomes more important than the meaning. I want to explore individual lives in order to discuss their leadership against research more generally into emotion, and place people within their organisations. The book is framed, to paraphrase Bottery (2004: 2), to help headteachers deal better with the emotions which surround them, emotions which affect the realisation of their visions of educational purpose.

My background

I was a teacher and a deputy headteacher. Later, I became a governor of primary and secondary schools. From this experience came my interest in professional support (Crawford, Edwards and Kydd, 1998), and later, leading in difficult circumstances (Crawford, 2002; 2003). My research carried out in primary schools in special measures emphasised the part that the headteacher can play in empowering staff in order to achieve transformational effects:

> As followers internalise the leader's vision, and trust and confidence in the leader are high, followers feel more confident and they develop a sense of working together as a team. (Crawford, 2002: 279)

In that research I also noted the emotional strain on those in leadership positions in difficult contexts. One headteacher stated:

> It's very tiring, the paperwork and the waking up at 5:15 am and thinking about things. It takes a huge amount out of you, and there is only so much energy and amount of time you can put in. (ibid.: 280)

This viewpoint made me consider what emotional strain might be like for other heads in different contexts. Headteachers, it seemed, could unwittingly support the idea of headteachers being of central importance in the school, and that ideal 'professional' behaviour is rational and carefully emotionally controlled. Both of these concepts were often held at great personal cost by headteachers. My earlier research had suggested that a rational ideal is an illusion, not just in terms of desirability but also in practice. These developing interests in headteachers as people led to this book.

Emotion

Why then is emotion so important, and why should it be important to headteachers in particular? The English school leader is held very accountable for the success or failure of their school through such markers as Ofsted and league tables. Other countries have a similar policy agenda that emphasises accountability. This accountability can be felt, as we saw above, as a very personal responsibility. Parents and the community may view the headteacher as the most important person in the school, responsible for their child's progress or lack of it. Because of such accountability, headship is an ever more demanding role. Gronn views the current climate for educational leadership as 'greedy work' (2003: 147), as it asks more and more of headteachers. As Shields aptly describes it:

> Educational leadership is widely recognised as complex and challenging. Educational leaders are expected to develop learning communities, build the professional capacity of teachers, take advice from parents, engage in collaborative and consultative discussion making, resolve conflicts, engage in educative instructional leadership, and attend respectfully, immediately, and appropriately to the needs and requests of families with diverse cultural, ethnic, and socioeconomic backgrounds. Increasingly, educational leaders are faced with tremendous pressure to demonstrate that every child for whom they are responsible is achieving success. (Shields, 2004: 109)

James describes how leading effective schools is facilitated by the headteacher's recognition and understanding of the environment created by emotions and the power of often subconscious emotion (James, 2000). A very helpful starting point for focusing on this area is that made by Denzin, who suggests why emotion is so important. He proposes that:

> Emotions cut to the core of people. Within and through emotion, people come to define the surface and essential, or core, meanings of who they are. (Denzin, 1984: 2)

This places a firm emphasis on emotion at the centre of personal understanding of self. Understanding of self can also be the key to understanding others and the relationships those others have with the headteacher. This can include staff, but also parents, students and the wider school environment. When thinking of the importance of emotion in relationships, I like the idea that:

> Our feelings signal to us, sometimes clearly, sometimes inchoately, something of the quality of our interactions, performances, and involvement in the world around us. (Newton, Handy and Fineman, 1995: 122)

In other words, how these feelings are embodied in personal practice is very important. Halpin talks of the operational image of the headteacher which echoes this. He notes 'the important psychological function that communicating positive invitational messages has for enabling individuals and groups to build and act on a shared vision of enhanced learning experiences for pupils' (2003: 77). I talk in more depth about this later in the book.

What is emotion?

A difficulty that arises when working in the area of emotion and educational leadership is that terms such as 'emotion', 'emotional' and 'feelings' are used different ways by different writers, depending on their perspective. Gerrod Parrot (2001) suggests that everyone knows what emotion is until they are asked to define it. The fluidity of this area is implicit in the usage of terms such as 'emotion' itself and the related words 'affect', 'emotionality', 'mood' and 'feeling'. The dilemma is also reflected in the broad characterisation of emotions as either positive or negative elements of organisational culture. Oatley and Jenkins explain this in a way that I find useful when they note that emotions:

> often have aspects that we do not completely understand. They can be mere beginnings of something vague and unformed, with meanings that only become clear as we express them to others. At the same time, we sense that emotions lie close to our most authentic selves. (2003: 350)

The power of emotion may be concerned with incompleteness or leading when we do not know the answer (Oatley and Jenkins, 2003: 282). Oatley and Jenkins suggest that emotions have two aspects that have a substantial effect on other mental processes – an informational, conscious part which understands the object of our emotions, and a second controlling part that has been constrained by evolution for coping with situations such as threats. An example of this is one of the comments made by a head in the study about classroom observation:

> Judging classroom performance can be up to 75 per cent emotional, and it's a subjective thing and subject to feeling. You have a sense of things when you walk into a classroom. You look at the kids and the eyes. It's like when you are a teacher; you can see when the light is switched on. I have concerns about teachers who just deliver but you can't fault them for it. I would rather see a connection to certain children – to find the key to that child. It's all about making connections, and not just thinking it is a job. They may go on to other paths in life from something that happened when you taught them – so it is a huge responsibility.

'Making connections' is all about emotion. In the psychological literature, the term 'affect' is often used to indicate this area, and I use it when a generic point is being made about emotional aspects of behaviour. So for a working definition, affect in schools is made up of:

- feelings (what we experience internally)
- emotions (feelings that we show)
- moods (feelings that persist over time).

Most of this book's focus will be on emotion, although feelings will play a part in the discussions. As one of the headteachers I talked to put it: 'Emotions are all about feelings. You get vibes. I can smell a rat at 50 yards.' However emotion is conceptualised, affect has a real and vital role to play not only in personal effectiveness as a headteacher/leader, but also in understanding leadership itself. This is because working together in groups has both a biological and a social component.

Getting to the heart of school leadership

Relationships with staff, pupils and parents, are quite literally at the *heart of* education (Sergiovanni, 2003). The headteacher is at the centre of these professional emotional relationships. Their *heart for* education sets the context for all the other important relationships in the school. This view resonates with the concept of the head as tribal leader, or carrier of culture suggested by Sergiovanni (1995), and his or her role as a social or moral agent (Murphy and Beck, 1994).

Such a focus on the headteacher might at first seem to be going against the grain of current educational leadership thinking, when there is so much emphasis in both research and policy-making on distributed leadership, and most recently, system leadership. Knowledge of emotion and leadership is relevant to all forms of leadership, because of the social aspect of the role, and the importance of influence. I would still argue that headship is a crucial factor in schools, where an effective headteacher may enable leadership in its distributed form. If their heart for education sets the context for all other personal relationships within schools, then the personal, emotional side of headship becomes one that is worth exploring further. Getting to the heart of leadership is therefore multifaceted, with the position of leader a crucial one in enabling leadership to be most effective for the educational purposes of schools.

Getting to the heart of leadership is an area which has become more popular in recent years. Emotional intelligence (EI), for example, has had a strong influence in schools (Goleman, 1995). EI, however, has inherent dangers for the practitioner in education – there are dangers of oversimplification in converting complex concepts into bite-sized competences. Fineman (2000: 277–8) argues that emotion can easily become just another topic, whilst emotionalising organisations means that we are more able to look for new understandings of situations. 'Emotionalising organisations' is part of the overall aim of this book. Bringing out new interpretations and understandings by understanding emotion is not just a competence of leaders, but is a lens through which to view leadership. In other words, I see emotion as inherent to the practice of leadership rather than separate from it. All organising actions are inseparable from and influenced by emotion.

Reclaiming leadership as a social and organisational process

Reading writings on leadership, you are often left with the idea that leaders act apart from the organisation.

Leadership is a social process (Bell and Harrison, 1995; Duke, 1998). It depends on the relationships that are built both within the school, and also in the wider community. From this social viewpoint, I feel it is insufficient to concentrate attention on either 'emotion' or 'leadership'. To understand school leadership more fully, the phrase 'emotion and leadership' as two separate terms, doesn't really help. As Francesca, an experienced headteacher, put it: 'Emotion is crucial to being able to interact with and understand other human beings. If you didn't have emotion it would make life incredibly difficult.'

Although the experience of work is drenched with emotion, it is often viewed as tangential rather than fundamental to leadership, but leadership cannot function without emotion. One head, Laura, told me:

> I class myself as an emotional person, because feelings are an important part of my leadership style. Emotion management in school is not about control. I aim to be positive and can control the raw stuff. I use that to move out of that feeling, and try to orchestrate those feelings towards something positive. I really believe that if you talk up, you feel up, and can talk yourself and others into becoming positive and buoyant.

In Chapter Nine I consider positive management.

Headship is framed within various contexts: the local and national context, the school context and the personal context – all of which influence the personal emotional response of the headteacher. Emotion is at once a personal quality of the headteacher, and at the same time a quality of the social relationships in the school. This book concentrates on the interplay between the two. Although the focus will often be on headteachers, I hope that the discussion will also interest those in any leadership position in schools.

Think points

Each chapter includes some think points to help you engage in greater detail with the ideas that are suggested. They focus on the relevance of what each chapter discusses to your leadership context. Before you read the rest of the book, you may like to try and unpick your own views on this sometimes sensitive and difficult area.

1 What is your current view of emotion and its relationship to leadership?
2 What has influenced this view? Be as specific as you can, recalling particular incidents.
3 Who has had the greatest impact on you emotionally in a work setting? Why?

Chapter 2

Perspectives on emotion and leadership

Introduction

In the next few chapters, I will examine in detail the stories of some particular headteachers, focusing on their biographies and emotional experiences. This focus can help to understand emotion and its impact on your own leadership stance. I will explore the importance of emotion and leadership, both for the practice of leadership in schools, and in terms of emotion within leadership studies more generally. Before moving on to stories of some head-teachers or 'narratives of headship', I want to look at some of the perspectives on emotion and leadership that I have found most helpful when conducting workshops with educational leaders. This will help explain why such narratives are important. The following is a 'taster' for this whole area, with ideas for you to follow, as you need to. I am going to suggest several frameworks from the liter-ature which I have used with headteachers, and ways in which they might be valuable to your own school leadership development. They are illustrated with examples from my research. At the end of the chapter, I'll make some suggestions for further reading, as well as suggesting some think points.

What do we need to know about emotion?

Much of the research into emotion looks at individual moti-vation and interpretation of events rather than emphasising the fixed and the predictable (Gerrod Parrott and Spackman, 2000). Briner summarises it helpfully:

> Emotion may come to be studied as a phenomenon that is somehow separate from behaviour and cognition at work: that we look at emotion as a new and separate aspect of work psychology. To take this approach would be a fundamental mistake as, to repeat the point I have made many times already, emotion is intrinsic to work behaviour and not a separate part of it ... For researchers and practitioners who are interested in emotion, a key task is to put emotion into what they are already doing, thereby helping to integrate emotion with their existing research and practice. If this is not done, the theoretical and practical relevance of emotion to almost every aspect of work behaviour will remain unexplored and emotion will once more become marginalized within work and organizational psychology. (1999: 342)

Briner argues for the integration of emotion within existing research and practice. This would seem to be an excellent aim for those that study leadership in schools. Rather than emotion being either, 'out there', to be acknowledged but not dealt with, or a subject only of interest to those con-cerned with emotional difficulties/troubles, my aim is to put emotion back into what you are already doing as a leader. One way to do this is by focusing on that connection to self through emotion as a leadership narrative.

The educational leadership literature currently suggests that emotion is an important part of leadership, although much of the work tends towards the social, external aspects of emotion. Interestingly, there is a lack of engagement in the educational leadership literature with the inherent, personal aspects of emotion. This is curious, because emotion is with leaders all the time, whether they acknowledge this consciously or not. As Damasio eloquently puts it, and from which I took this book's epigraph:

> But there they are, feelings of myriad emotions and related states, the continuous musical lines of our minds, the unstoppable humming of the most universal of melodies that only dies down when we go to sleep. (Damasio, 2004: 3)

Headteachers are emotional beings but this is not always readily apparent in the educational leadership literature. The difficulty for those in headship positions is to acknowledge the personal, to somehow look at the 'continuous musical lines of our minds' in ways that enhance personal effectiveness and help manage any inner anxiety. Fineman describes this as making 'the connection between feeling, body and social meaning' (2003: 16). The educational leadership literature rarely considers headship from the perspective of the headteacher – in other words, 'what does it feel like to be in that role?' This is probably because such subjectivity is viewed in an accountability culture as suspect. I would argue that understanding the emotions of leadership is a key to long-term sustainability and high functioning in headship. To me this seems a much more valid and useful approach.

Personal biography and personal meanings meet in the cultural and organisational perspective of the school. This meeting shapes emotional expression in the school, not just with the staff but pupils, parents and the wider community. Understanding emotion can support what school leaders do. This is often in ways of which they are not always conscious. Before turning to some of those ways that emotion can be looked at, it is worth briefly mentioning the area of gender and emotion, as it is often one of the first areas that comes up for discussion when looking at emotion and leadership.

Gender and emotion

Both gender and emotion are overarching concepts. Gender stereotypes would have us believe that men are rational and cool, and therefore superior. Women are irrational, emotional, too personal, and thus inferior. If we sometimes discuss emotion in terms of the rational/irrational divide, so it can also be characterised in terms of a gender divide. Social values and gender stereotypes (Sachs and Blackmore, 1998) can serve to make the rational approach seem superior. Harnessing emotion as a way to present ideas, or reach conclusions, is not seen as legitimate. Blackmore argues that looking at women in leadership specifically too often makes women the problem rather than problematising the concept of leadership within the wider context of power and gender relations (1999: 6). Another way of dealing with this is to refuse to separate the public and private faces of emotion, or in other words the emotional context. Blackmore (1999: 164–5) has argued that when women display what might be viewed as unprofessional, non-rational negative emotions, for example anger, they can be viewed as uncaring. If they cry they are seen as weak. Women can be trapped into the positive aspects of emotion such as warmth, care and patience and (at the same time) have to manage the negative emotions of others. As Blackmore puts it, they must be both 'vulnerable and strong' (ibid.: 165). This dilemma was illustrated strongly by Hillary Clinton's presidential campaign in 2007–08.

Coleman (2002: 82) notes that women can feel exposed as leaders because of preconceptions and expectations that the leader will be male. The female headteachers that Sachs and Blackmore interviewed wanted to be professional and the professional face, marked by absence of emotion, was part of how they defined their professionalism. Some feminist writers argue that writing about the emotional dimension of school life and leadership is one of the great silences of organisational analysis in education, where people value 'headwork over heartwork' (Sachs and Blackmore, 1998: 270). Men also have to work within an emotional context. Sachs and Blackmore argue that men may in fact put up with more from the impact of restrictive expectations on their means of doing emotional work – 'effective leadership is also about, or requires managing emotions or making emotions visible' (1998: 265). Finally, in discussing over-arching gender issues which relate to emotion, it is relevant to note Beatty's work, especially in the way she defines 'the notion of a professional fragmented self' (Beatty, 2002: 110), as an issue for headteachers, particularly female ones. Both men and women can learn a great deal by reflecting on the inner emotional experiences of leadership as part of their professional growth and to help sustain them in headship. The issue of sustainability in headship is looked at in more detail in Chapter Eight.

Ways of looking at emotion

To begin to get to the heart of leadership, I am now going to suggest one way of thinking, or conceptual framework, from the differing perspectives on emotion. The idea that you can consciously reflect on your emotional state at any one time is a useful one for headteachers, but it is made easier if there is a particular focus of that reflection. My main aim is to pull out aspects that have the greatest practical use for those in leadership positions in schools, and which allow leaders in education to focus on some of the most important aspects of the study of emotion that are relevant to education. Inevitably, in such a large area, there are aspects that will not be explored in this book, which may be particularly relevant to you. Each chapter has further reading to help you find out more, should you wish to.

The original architects of emotional intelligence (EI), Salovey and Mayer talk about approaching what they called 'life tasks', with what they call emotional intelligence (Salovey and Mayer, 1990; 2001). These four processes are:

1 appraisal and expression of emotion (self and others)
2 regulation of emotion
3 utilisation of emotion
4 emotion's facilitation of thinking.

Salovey and Meyer considered it important that individuals were able to apply these processes to emotional content in social situations. This meant assessing their own feelings, and that of others, accurately. You can see the particular application to leadership, which is the direction Goleman followed later that has struck a chord with many leaders. The way that the mind operates is beyond the scope of this book, but one of their useful suggestions is that emotion helps the processing of information, and helps people develop multiple options in any given situation. They argue that this leads to a high level of emotional reasoning and knowledge, which is where the application to educational leaders becomes pertinent. They can use such knowledge in interpersonal relationships. This blend of mind and emotion, the rational and non-rational is important to note, because of the tendency in any discussion of emotion to adopt either one position or the other.

Deborah Lupton (1998) has produced a way of looking at emotions that avoids setting up a divide. Drawing on the discourses people use when they discuss emotion, she suggests that you can view approaches to emotion under two broad tendencies. First, there is 'emotions as inherent' and concerned with the self. This helps you to focus on what it is about you that is driving particular feelings. Second, you can view 'emotions as socially constructed', which helps you to concentrate on what is happening in any given situation. Lupton emphasises that this distinction has a significant degree of overlap, and should be viewed more as a continuum. Most work in the educational leadership area concentrates on emotions as socially constructed. This could be because this focus has more instant, practical applications. Also, it can be much more difficult and challenging to look at yourself, or ask others to help you do so. As Lupton notes:

> It is important not to take a too relativistic approach to the emotions, neglecting their sensual, embodied nature ... the emotional self is always also an embodied self, for it is inevitably through the body that we construct, live, and make sense of emotion. (1998: 10)

For each leader, their own bodily feelings will be unique, and effective leaders read these signs as an important part of emotional management. Given that there is so much that an educational leader might need to grasp, there are several starting points that I want to suggest.

Textures

When I first began to look at this area, the variety of theoretical approaches to the study of emotion was enriching yet diverse. EI, for example, is a popular concept for many reasons, and surely partly because it is relatively easy to understand its practical implications for leaders in schools. Other approaches also have value for the educational leader but may be more difficult to explore at first sight. I have used the idea of *emotional textures* – inspired by a section name in Fineman's book, *Emotion in Organizations* (2000) – when working with educational leaders as a means of introduction to the entire area. The word 'textures' made me think more about the richness and multiplicity of emotion and educational leadership in particular. Textures means acknowledging how closely emotion and educational leadership are linked. They are a way to get to the heart of your own personal leadership journey. I'll discuss how they relate to each other at the end of the chapter.

The three textures are:

- emotional regulation in educational leadership
- emotion-weighted decision-making in educational leadership
- emotional context in educational leadership.

Dictionaries define textures in various ways, but most definitions emphasise that a texture reveals something typical and distinctive about something complex. Emotions are inherent and socially constructed. For me, the idea of textures helps in capturing some of the essence of emotion as it relates to leadership.

Emotional regulation in educational leadership

Goffman (1961) proposed that every kind of social interaction is like a game in which we take on roles. We can become more or less strongly engaged in a role. Fulfilment is more likely to occur when we are fully engaged in a role. This can, of course, lead to tensions. When the role we are being asked to play as a leader grates against our innermost values, huge personal strain can occur. Schools are often places where the management or control of emotion is played out against a script of what a leader *should* do. The strain of 'performance' can have a negative effect on leadership, the joy of performance a positive effect. A key study in this area is that of Arlie Hochschild (1983) who studied the role of emotion management in the life of flight attendants. She explored the tensions that build up when an individual has to give a particular performance as part of their job. So, airline hostesses for Delta had to make passengers feel welcome onboard, and were constantly exhorted to smile. She called this, 'emotional labour', where workers may be required to simulate or suppress feelings, so that others had a 'good' emotional experience. Just like Hochschild's flight attendants who had to fake emotions they did not feel, so headteachers may have to put on what they believe to be the appropriate emotion for a headteacher. Hochschild argued that, over a longer period, this way of managing, created lost capacity to listen to our feelings, and sometimes even to feel at all (1983: 21).

There is potential for a huge disconnection between shown emotion and private feeling in education, but the stress of emotional labour can be overstated as well. The headteachers I interviewed were sometimes positively gleeful when they talked animatedly about playing a role – examples such as 'I put on my eyes and teeth' (Francesca), 'acting the clown' (Laura), 'Must make sure you are not leaking!' (Eleanor) can be viewed like this. One new headteacher, Ben, seemed to find it useful and perhaps comforting in terms of his own self and self-esteem to 'play' the role of head. Fineman puts it this way 'Some are more than content to 'fake in good faith' in the service drama' (Fineman, 2000: 5). How a headteacher manages the boundaries between 'faking in good faith' and excessive emotional labour is one of the things we will look at in Chapter Seven.

Dollard et al. (2003: 84) suggest that human service work has some unique aspects. They note that in direct person-related jobs, such as teaching, nursing and social work, each employee is fully responsible for high quality and satisfactory service delivery, unlike in a factory where problems can be fixed before reaching the customer. Customers can have particular expectations and behaviours, or organisational customer perceptions (OCP) which are a further source of stress (ibid.: 85). Headteachers, particularly those in primary schools, could be seen to be at the sharp end of OCP, but schools in general often struggle with outdated perceptions of their academic performance, which may be rooted in the past. At the time of writing, primary headship vacancies were running at a much higher level than secondary ones, perhaps in part due to this closeness to the players in the drama of school. As well as emotional labour, human service work involves customer-related social stressors (CSS), Dollard suggests. These operate on an individual level during what they call employee–customer interactions. In schools, the notion of the customer could be broadened to include pupils, parents and staff. Again, primary school leaders are more likely to experience the pressure of this sort of interaction on a daily basis.

Stress

Hochschild and others have argued that it is only when *emotional dissonance* occurs that stress becomes an issue. What does that mean? It's the frequent need to display positive emotions that are not the same as the neutral or negative emotions that you are actually feeling. This continuous display can be associated with ill health, because eventually individuals suffering with emotional dissonance lose the capability to regulate their own emotion, and can become unable to work. This capacity for self-regulation is an important internal resource. Without it, work-related stress is more likely to occur. The further readings at the end of this chapter will give you ways of exploring the concept of regulation further. On a cautionary note, Oatley and Jenkins (2003) remind us that regulation can be a confusing idea. That's because in the literature it is used to discuss patterns of emotion (for example, intense anger), as well as how we can amend our expression of emotion (for example, distracting ourselves). They suggest that, 'Some individuals for reasons of up-bringing, or genetics, or both, come to have a bias towards experiencing and expressing certain emotions more than others' (2003: 121). This is an important point to note in the context of educational leadership, and the life stories in the next few chapters. I will be suggesting that better awareness of your own bias in expressing emotion helps you to understand the amount of emotional labour that you may need for some aspects of leadership in schools.

The ability to 'play' the role of headteacher is linked to the emotional health of the organisation as a whole. Argyris (1996; 1999) views organisations that function well as psy-chologically safe, but suggests that it is much more common for organisations to be places where relationships are super-ficial and wary. If this is the case in a school, knowledge of the emotional regulation that might be needed could help a new headteacher approach the task with more confidence. Specific ideas such as the recognition and classification of dissonance are not really leadership tools in themselves. They can, however, make leaders aware of the powerful nature of their own emotions, and how this can in turn influence those they work with. For example, if a school wishes to be psychologically safe for its headteacher, I would suggest it is an organisation that has a growing awareness of the role of emotions in educational leadership.

Emotions as they are discussed in everyday usage are powerful *essences* of organisations. They can help leaders understand more of what is happening underneath the surface of day-to-day interaction. Sometimes they are expressed, but can be just as powerful unexpressed. It has been suggested (Pekrun and Frese, 1992) that positive and negative emotions can be usefully classified into social- and task-related emotions. So, in a school, for example, social emotions may make up what could be described as the mood of the organisation. These sorts of emotions can be looked at separately from task-related emotions. This background of social emotion will influence any task-related issue. Tasks happen within the context of social emotions although they may be unexpressed most of the time by, for example, the teachers. Staff will also draw upon their cognitive ability to examine how helpful these emotions are. People's cognitive ability will also allow them to understand what prospective emotions may arise in the future from a similar situation.

Emotions are also socially experienced, which involves relationships. Bodily changes ('My palms went sweaty and my mouth dry but I tried not to show that I was afraid') may or may not give signals that the person involved in any social relationship is emotionally stimulated. Leaders may have one view of what is professionally correct, and labour to present that face. The emotional cost of such labour can be considerable in terms of stress within the organisation. Sometimes, as in the schools in special measures that I discussed in Chapter One, the required emotion is too hard to manage. In an emotionally safe school, headteachers need to be able to call upon personal reserves in times of crisis, and enable their staff to express their own feelings and emotions in a way that is helpful to them and to the school as a whole.

Can it be done?

It is clear that there is potential for a huge disconnection between shown emotion and private feeling, but the stress of emotional labour can be overstated as well. Those who interact with the public professionally, such as headteachers, have a 'professional/rational' part of themselves on display most of the time. This containment and regulation is necessary for the smooth running of schools. All the headteachers I talked to were entirely conscious that there were times when they had to 'act the headteacher'. Often these were the times when they wanted to raise the spirits of others, or alter the mood in a specific setting. As one male head put it:

> Your emotions, if not handled, might slip out somewhere else and colour your relationship with another person. It's all to do with how something might be affecting someone else. For example, there's a child at school with a serious condition for whom the longer-term prognosis is poor. This affects the whole staff. As a head, you have to not take things to heart. You need to be more philosophical, learning not to take things personally. As a person, I know that I am easily moved by emotional events.

He notes that extreme feelings could not be managed in such a way. Several headteachers talked about the fact that it was important that others knew when they felt such distress. They were able to admit to very difficult feelings, such as grief. However, shame and anxiety, which might reflect on them as a 'competent' headteacher, were more difficult to handle. Of great interest, I think, is that they were also aware of the times when they needed to have someone in whom to confide, either inside or outside the school. Finding that non-judgmental emotional outlet could be difficult at times for them.

For headteachers I talked to, emotion and its management in day-to-day interactions was never far away. Headteachers, especially in primary schools, often act as a conduit for others' emotions. In the context of young children in primary schools, emotional expression is never too far away and it is a natural part of work with younger children. This may mean that primary heads are left feeling more vulnerable overall, and could be one reason for the current shortage of applicants: in primary schools, perhaps as one primary head noted, 'If the head[teacher] is not calm, the school is not calm.'

Understanding the role of emotion in leadership

George (2000) argues strongly from work carried out in neurology, that the evidence suggests that feelings are necessary to make good decisions. Whilst very intense emotions may make decision-making more difficult, an intense reduction in emotion may also lead to irrational behaviour. Emotional management does not mean suppression of feelings, as this may lead to greater emotional dissonance, and what we like to call stress. Relevant work on stress (Cooper, Dewe and O'Driscoll, 2001) suggests that this may be the case. Revealing feelings to others in a group is very little emphasised in educational leadership texts. Work in psychology (Hess and Kirouac, 2004) suggests that paying close attention to displays of emotion is very important. It provides information on several levels – how the person is feeling, how they see the world and how they relate to others. Hess and Kirouac give a very helpful example. If someone is angry, it not only tells us that the person feels wronged, but it can also help inform leaders in other ways – 'an anger display signals dominance and can be considered informative regarding the relative power of the anger expressing individual' (2004: 368).

In my study, heads saw the power of displays of emotion, whether real or put on for the benefit of the other party. Several of the stories they told me (for example, Eleanor dealing with a difficult site manager, James and the difficult interview with a parent, Mary and the incompetent supply teacher) told of this kind of emotional management. They also agreed that they did not ever want to be seen as out of control emotionally, but wanted to discuss ways in which they could flag up emotions such as anger to others in the school. Mary and the incompetent teacher is a good example of this.

Mary and the supply teacher

Fineman and others (Oatley and Jenkins, 2003) remind us that shame and embarrassment are two key features of social control. Mary, a very experienced primary head, gave me a very detailed account of an incident in her school. She felt it had drained her emotionally.

I had received parental complaints about a temporary member of staff not allowing children to use the toilet, so I spoke to the teacher about school policy, but the teacher said she did not agree with it. In fact, she said she was 'adamant'. This interview took place in my office, and I told her she had to conform to school policy. After I had established the facts, and heard the teacher's hard line, I felt quite angry and also nervous. My own daughter was in this class and during one break arrived at my door distraught and wet, because she had been kept in and not allowed to go to the toilet. I got someone to look after her, and went to see the teacher straight away. The teacher was brought up to the office for an explanation. She said that she was making an example of children who had not learnt their spelling. I explained that this was not school policy, and certainly not part of the spelling strategy. I told the teacher that the children were so frightened that they couldn't learn, and that she must stop it immediately. I also told her that I was very angry. I was now very concerned, so I began observations of lessons. The teacher was told when this would take place, and had to give in planning beforehand. What I saw was awful, and I can describe it as really a 'holding operation'. I went back a week later, and found the work set was now too difficult. The teacher challenged the feedback – 'I feel you are doing this on purpose, challenging me'. The attached inspector was then invited in. Observations were done across the whole school and work sampling in the year group. It was obvious that levels in this teacher's class were not appropriate. There were more observations by the attached inspector. During the feedback, the teacher became very angry. She shouted, 'I don't know what this bloody woman wants!' and ran out of the school. The situation moved to capability. There were targets and observations for three weeks. The teacher went off with stress for six months. I got an occupational health assessment and the teacher didn't come back. I had to teach the class myself for a term because of the disruption. I felt frustration and anger together. I also was disappointed that the teacher could not be helped. I feel that I would have acted quicker if my own daughter had not been in the class.

In Mary's story overall she is emotional in pursuit of a rational management objective – to have the best teacher in front of that class. The telling of this story really illustrates the dilemma of the affective/rational interface. Mary had to work very hard with suppressing her own feelings. Her own values, and what she believed about education and social justice were deeply involved in her recall of the situation, as well as having to separate the roles of parent (emotion of a mother) and headteacher even more than is usual. This caused even more emotional labour for Mary.

When emotional management is this conscious, it is part of the headteacher's day-to-day leadership practice. It may rely for its very effectiveness on the fact that it is managed. When headteachers are no longer able to manage and regulate feelings, perhaps because their inner self is compromised, then stress and ultimately breakdown are the more likely to occur.

The story of the supply teacher also illustrates emotion-weighted decision-making, another key aspect of leadership in schools.

Emotion-weighted decision-making in leadership

Having researched primary schools in special measures, one of the notable features was the pivotal emotional figure of the headteacher in the school. Yet, today, we are much more likely to talk of distributed leadership in schools. There are contradictions between accountability and distributed leadership, and I wondered whether there was some emotional explanation. What leadership and emotional function does an educational leader need to exercise that was not so important for a class teacher and where emotion might play an underrated part? Emotion-weighted decision-making is a pivotal part of the headteachers' role, and might help explain this.

Decision-making links to an important property of emotion because, as Oatley and Jenkins have argued (2003: 82), emotions arise in our daily lives largely in terms of problems to be solved. Put simply, most emotions can be said to be 'about' something. The popularity of emotional intelligence (EI) as a framework may be because of its relationship to the 'aboutness' of emotion. EI implicitly suggests that emotion and decision-making is mainly a competence that can be learnt. There are many circumstances around decision-making in schools where emotion is heightened. It has been suggested (Earley and Weindling, 2004) that the interest in emotional intelligence is really part of a quest for superior performance in leadership. The point that I'm making is that self-awareness is more than just a competence. The EI/competence route in educational leadership could be seen as a 'short cut' to effectiveness rather than part of an overall understanding of emotion and leadership.

Decision-making is most often conceptualised as a rational process in educational leadership texts. The competing strands of an organisation's life cannot be ordered and controlled. This is developed in the business literature, particularly in the work of Fineman (2000, 2001, 2003, 2005). Fineman proposes that the idea of the rational organisation as a place where emotion can be controlled out of existence is a naïve assumption by those who manage (Fineman, 2001). He argues (2000: 10) that the management is about order, and this ordering is actually carried out by using emotional preferences and emotionalising our understandings of situations. For example, in decision-making in leadership roles, leaders may view the process as having been carried out rationally, in neat steps. Fineman suggests (2003) that this view is emotionally infused. Decision-making is portrayed as rational in retrospect, but is often an unfolding, conflictual process. He advocates the view that there is a Western tendency to rationalise our emotions, and make them look unemotional, as emotion is not seen as a legitimate way of either presenting ideas, or suggesting how we reached conclusions (2000: 96). He also notes that social values and gender stereotypes reinforce this viewpoint. It could be compelling to suggest that we could somehow read the runes of emotion in order to restore rationality by managing our own feelings better. What Fineman proposes is that because we want to think and believe that what we are doing is rational, we create social discourses that define how we ought to feel and display emotion. Justifying how one behaves emotionally in a social situation in school can be termed 'professional behaviour'. He defines rationality as the presentation of emotionalised processes so that they are acceptable to others. This may be what many leaders in schools attempt to do. Fineman's view is that feelings and emotions lubricate, rather than impair rationality. You may like to explore more of this work in the further readings at the end of the chapter.

Ginsberg and Davies (2002), in their research on educational decision-making, argue that whatever kind of leadership is being exercised, leaders have to make decisions, and live with the consequences. One of the conclusions of their research is that educational leaders are rarely prepared in their training for leadership for the deeply emotional experiences that will occur in their schools. In their writings they suggest:

> While it is often 'lonely at the top' for leaders, it seems unhealthy and counter-productive to be isolated when making difficult decisions … [they wonder] whether some case-based training, further emphasis in MBA or educational leadership programs or creating avenues for leaders to share their concerns with peers could be beneficial. (Ginsberg and Gray Davies, 2002: 279)

A focus on the leader's feelings, and therefore a less 'rational' approach, is also a feature of the work of Ackerman and Maslin-Ostrowski (2004). They talk about the fact that there are leadership events that leave 'wounds'. Many of the day-to-day decisions of headship may cause emotional fallout, and headteachers have to learn what to do about this. In schools, the leader's understanding of how someone's inner world may have a profound impact on the school setting is a key skill, but at the same time they have to allow room for self-understanding. This is because leadership is an important and essential component that helps emotionally sustain organisations.

Emotional context in leadership

Emotional context is more than the social context of the

school, because emotional context is also created by the internal state of the participants. You could argue that the other two textures that have been discussed above can be subsumed within the idea of emotional context. That is because the idea of emotional context applies to the leader, the followers, and the social context they create together. I have already briefly examined one of the most influential books of recent times, *Emotional Intelligence* (Goleman, 1995). Goleman argues that the emotionally intelligent have abilities in five main domains: they know their emotions, manage their emotions, motivate themselves, recognise emotion in others and handle relationships (1995: 43–4). This way of looking at emotions has been helpful to many, and helped place emotions as a legitimate area for discussion, especially in regard to leadership. The dangers with this 'emotional intelligence' approach have been noted by several writers (Beatty, 2002; Fineman, 2000). Fineman suggests that Goleman promises a form of rationality that is at best illusory. As an approach it is aimed at managerial behaviours. The idea of emotional context takes a different view of emotion and leadership as it suggests that you need to look at the whole culture of the organisation, and the values of its stakeholders. The idea of connectedness with others in the organisational setting also assumes greater importance, because organisation theory suggests that the individual has a need for coherence between themselves and the social context.

How can you discover the emotional context?

It is in the emotional context that definitions of emotional meaning take place. I would argue that part of the leader's role is to help define those meanings. The emotional context of the school will draw on inherent emotions in staff, parents and children, and the way they manage outward displays of emotion in a school context. The headteacher is at the centre of much of this creation of emotional meaning. Within the emotional context, all the other aspects of leadership and management (finance, curriculum, etc.) take place.

People convey their feelings about the affective quality of relationships at work very indirectly. It is often through stories. Stories are a way to understand emotional meaning in the workplace, and enable discussions of difficult areas, and the next chapter will look at this idea in more detail. As researchers have put it:

> When we ask where is feeling in people's accounts of work, we find it not in statements of feeling but in stories about work … stories invite readers into the workplace, to see and feel what workers see and feel. (Sandelands and Boudens, 2000: 55)

The emotional context can only be partially understood through stories, but they are often a means for the educational leader to begin to understand that context. Understanding their own story is crucial too. It has been proposed that the issue that makes the central and defining task of managing people so complex is that the manager/leader must bring his/her person/self to the role (Hirschhorn, 1997). One of the key connectors between emotion and leadership is managing oneself within a network of relationships. The next chapter begins to explore some of the ways in which narratives can help headteachers understand that emotional context more fully.

Think points

1 Jot down the three emotions that most readily come to mind when you think of your leadership role. Try to see whether they are inherent, social or a mixture of both.
2 Can you think of a situation that you have experienced which could be said to involve gender and emotion? Relating it to this chapter, what are the key learning points?
3 How useful to you as an idea is 'emotional labour'? Can you think of a specific example from school?
4 How conscious are you of how your body handles emotion? What does it tell you about your own bias towards experiencing and expressing emotion?
5 Describe the current emotional context of your school, and how it influences you as a leader.

Further reading

If you are interested in some of the ideas that are mentioned in this chapter, you may like to look at some of the original work. Each of these readings gives more insight into the theories used to study emotion and how they relate to leadership.

Ackerman, R. and Maslin-Ostrowski, P. (2004) 'The wounded leader and emotional learning in the school-house', *School Leadership and Management*, 24 (3): 311–28.
This article is very useful for understanding how deep emotional experiences can profoundly change the nature of leadership in a very personal way.

Fineman, S. (ed.) (2008) *The Emotional Organization*. Oxford: Blackwell.
This book clearly relates emotion to the values and social identity of an organisation. Although none of the examples

are school-specific, they provide much food for thought for school leaders.

Gronn, P. (2003) *The New Work of New Educational Leaders: Changing Leadership Practice in an Era of School Reform.* London: Paul Chapman.
As well as looking at aspects of emotion, this book discusses the policy framework and shows how this has meant that leaders are often swallowed up by the demands made on them.

Hochschild, A.R. (1983) *The Managed Heart: Commercialization of Human Feeling.* Berkeley: University of California Press.
This is a classic book for anyone who is interested in the original research and how Hochschild developed the idea of emotional labour. It is both highly readable and intellectually stimulating.

Lupton, D. (1998) *The Emotional Self.* London: Sage.
Lupton's book can take you further if you are interested in the wider aspects of how research into emotion is conceptualised.

Chapter 3

Narratives – the emotional power of storytelling

Introduction

This chapter outlines the nature of my research, and my interest in narratives. It begins to introduce the headteachers that I worked with in more detail, so that you can see the emotional context in which their narrative is told. It does this by introducing the idea of a personal leadership narrative as a tool for self-development in emotion and leadership. The personal leadership narrative of the headteacher and the organisation's 'emotional histories' built up over time from everyday interactions, are both important. These narratives influence the interpretation of events by everyone involved in the emotional context of the school.

Developing a personal leadership narrative

The idea of a narrative is one that is often helpful when looking at emotion and headteachers. Briner maintains that, 'Emotion occurs in the context of our personal narrative – our history, present and anticipated future' (1999: 337). Our history makes up our personal leadership narrative, that depends on emotional involvement and recall. In headship research, the link between emotion and personal narrative has been taken up by several authors in primary schooling (Pascal and Ribbins, 1998; Southworth, 1995). In David Loader's study (1997) of his professional life as an Australian college principal, he uses the narrative, story-telling approach. He cites the personal as being very important in being an effective leader. In fact, he argues (ibid.: 145) that personal reflection and a level of revelations in interactions with other school leaders could provide new insights into situations and allow conversations to have more meaning for those involved in school improvement. Details of these arguments can be found in the further readings at the end of the chapter.

Stories can help people overcome any difficulties they may have with whether it is professionally acceptable to discuss feelings. What gives such stories their power is how they touch upon the concerns of the teller emotionally, as I hope to draw out. They can also touch us, and relate to our own leadership narrative. Our feelings often are encased in the stories we tell, and more importantly these stories give legitimacy to our feelings (Fineman, 2003). As Fineman notes, 'The story is not a measure of the objective truth of an event, but is a fine indicator of our feelings and how we wish to present them' (2003: 17). Stories resonate in different ways with different people. They can also have diverse and even contradictory meanings for a single person (Gabriel, 2000: 90). All the stories told here and in the original research are intense, and have an emotional purpose. The meaning of all of them will be different for each reader, as good stories can possess many meanings. When you read the stories, you will be putting your own background, history and experiences behind the headteachers' own words.

Emotion is linked to leadership in many significant ways, through past events, through talk, through the personal sense of self, and in the culture of schools and schooling. All of this is linked to the part that emotion plays in our life events, and how they are played out in our individual memory. I would suggest that we don't look at the leadership narratives as memories as such, but much more as stories that people use to make sense of situations. I think a good summary of this way of looking at leaders in schools can be summed up by Roberts when he acknowledges that individual lives are full of 'ambiguity and incompleteness' (2002: 80).

Great care was taken to retain the original story and meaning, which is why I asked every headteacher to verify and authorise each account. In particular, I wanted to engage with the idea of storytelling, and how a response to storytelling can be not to challenge the facts but rather to engage with the meaning. As Gabriel says of his accounts collected from various organisations:

> Many [accounts] … are highly charged narratives, not merely recounting 'events', but interpreting them, enriching them, enhancing them, and infusing them with meaning … such accounts can be seen as an attempt to re-create reality *poetically*. (2000: 31)

This poetic element is important because leadership narratives can be told in many different ways. The headteachers in this book used their own life history to engage in building up their leadership narrative, and so are told and retold by people over time. Each account sits within a personal context but also within a much wider context of society. Goodley et al. (2004, Preface) argue that although narratives bring together the individual and their social lives they are 'always politicised, structured, cultured and socialised.' The leadership narratives of headteachers need to be viewed within a greater policy agenda, and I will return to this in Chapter Eight. First, let me place the stories within their research context.

How were the stories collected?

The stories we tell are of crucial importance in investigating emotion and the headteacher. Narrative works on many different levels, and as such has great potential, but can also be challenging to use in research. The use of narrative does help move away from simple cause and effect in emotion and leadership. Leadership itself grows from a complex interaction between identity, memory, temperament and emotion, and experience and training. As Beatty clearly puts it:

> Emotions are messy. As you begin to reflect upon them, they change. Emotional memory is difficult to rate for reliability. Emotions do not submit easily to quantitative or qualitative analysis. (2002: 120)

How leaders make a difference is also a messy process. The stories that are told in this book suggest that without emotion, there is no such thing as leadership. Instead of viewing these as separate, a personal leadership narrative allows for a more holistic approach, viewing each leader as a person bringing individual components to the role.

When I carried out the interviews, I drew on the work of Irving Seidman (1998). Seidman suggests that interviewing is very often the best way to proceed if researchers are interested in the life experiences of people and the meaning that they take from those experiences. He allows for a sequence of three interviews. He describes this as follows:

> People's behaviour becomes meaningful and understandable when placed in the context of their lives and the lives of those around them. … The first interview establishes the context of the participants' experience. The second allows participants to reconstruct the details of their

experience within the context in which it occurs. And the third encourages the participants to reflect on the meaning their experience holds for them. (1998: 11)

It is the reflection on meaning that can be particularly useful for leaders in education. How has the leadership narrative that you tell to yourself and others been influenced by personal and social emotion? In order to tell your own story in a way that will be most effective to your sustainability as a leader, you need listeners who are able to reflect on that meaning with you. A leadership narrative will take place within the leader's life story. It will contain specific critical moments when emotion and leadership come together in ways that often cause leaders to reframe their own leadership narrative in terms of emotion.

Critical moments

Part of the interviews that I conducted involved talking about specific emotional events. The term critical incident, moment or event can be used in a variety of ways. The overall idea of a critical incident and its analysis is that a detailed event can reveal a significant insight into a person or situation. By asking the heads to tell me about a specific emotional event, I hoped to gain insight into their emotional frame of reference for the incident. As part of the interviews, all of the headteachers were asked to reflect on two incidents from school. They had to involve either strong positive or negative emotion, so that it had lodged in their memory. The description of the incident and a reflection on it offered them an opportunity to look in more depth at the physical and mental components of the emotions involved. The story of Mary and the supply teacher in the last chapter is one example of such a story. Mary noted that the actual retelling of the story to me took her back inside, in terms of how she felt, as she told the story. She said that the feeling of anger that she had experienced at the time came back to the surface as she spoke. This is important to note because the telling of a leadership narrative with a strongly negative emotional component can have consequences for the teller that may or may not be helpful. A skilled listener needs to be able to judge whether this retelling is causing the teller to engage in an unhelpful struggle with the past or a conscious discussion of events that have great personal meaning. Instead of saying that the telling of a leadership narrative is an easy one to embark upon, we need to acknowledge that there are areas where specific help may be needed in order to tackle very difficult emotional incidents. However, most leaders or potential leaders in education can start with telling their life story and move on from there to locate and identify the threads that come together to make up their own personal leadership narrative.

Self and identity

An area that is linked to the idea of the leadership narrative is the concept of self, and how much about ourselves we are willing to reveal to the social groups we work with. The concept of self too is hotly debated, and is another area you can explore in further reading. In terms of getting to the heart of leadership, I think it is useful to link self and identity as a way of explaining events, even if the idea of identity is also a controversial issue. Briefly, I want to mention some ideas about memory, personality and how this links to identity. Ideas for further reading if this particularly interests you are given at the end of the chapter.

Research by Haviland-Jones and Kahlbaugh (2004) has shown that emotion may be very important in constructing identity, because emotions and thoughts are the things that are most real to people at any given moment. This approach to identity views emotional events as the 'glue of identity' (ibid.: 301). In terms of a personal leadership narrative, one of the functions of emotion is to glue together chunks of experience to provide meaning to what is happening. Theorists (for example, Gerrod Parrott and Spackman, 2000) suggest that memory is a huge part of thinking because so many things that are useful to us, such as perception, judgement and problem solving, rely on us being able to think back over what has happened in the past. Memory can thus be affected by emotion and emotion by memory. The link between memory and motivation is also very important for the idea of a personal leadership narrative, because I am suggesting that the process of recall can change a person's motivation – 'memories can be actively recruited to maintain, alter, or reinforce a person's mood, goals and plans' (ibid.: 482). The personal leadership narrative is in the tradition of the narrative perspective (Singer and Salovey, 1996) which sees people placing themselves within their own life story. Singer and Salovey suggest that we all have 'self-defining' memories, which we use to understand ourselves more generally. By looking at life goals overall and recalling positive memories, leaders can be more aware of the role that memory plays in emotion and their own leadership.

Personality and temperament

It has been proposed (Oatley and Jenkins, 2003: 216) that many parts of our personality are both emotional and social, and that there is continuity in our personalities over time. Each person will have their own individual inbuilt bias to behave in certain ways, which will be affected by many factors. Oatley and Jenkins note (2003: 218) that theorists tend to picture personality in five broad areas, some of which have an obvious emotional component:

1 neuroticism (anxiety, hostility and depression)
2 extraversion (warmth, positive emotions)
3 openness (to feelings and ideas)
4 agreeableness (trust, straightforwardness and compliance)
5 conscientiousness (achievement, self-striving and usefulness).

I have found that temperament, as a concept, is useful when discussing how people change and develop over time emotionally within relationships. It is little used today in leadership discussions probably because it's mistakenly allied with ideas about only certain people being 'born to lead'. This is a shame as there are many uses for the concept of temperament when looking at personal development, especially in the area of emotion and leadership. So what is temperament? Different writers have different views over the relationship of emotion to temperament. Oatley and Jenkins define temperament as:

> Those aspects of behaviour and emotions that are constitutional, that are stable over time and across situations, that have a neurophysiologic underpinning and that have some degree of heritability. (2003: 209)

They argue that temperament is important as an aspect of a person's emotional pattern through life that has a biological base, and will continue to affect choices that people make. We all know instinctively that some people seem 'more emotional' by temperament. One of the areas I explored in my research was the idea that there were some emotions in their leadership narrative that were stable over time. The headteachers found this a useful way of looking at their career and the choices they had made.

Epstein (1998) suggested that the self-concept is important to understand because it both changes with experience and at the same time organises that experience. Getting to the heart of leadership is also about understanding how peoples' theories about themselves as individuals are important to leadership. How we perceive ourselves is at the heart of leadership, and I have argued that there is a strong emotional component to this perception of self. At the same time, it is important to note that all of us 'resonate to theories that reflect our own interpretation of ourselves' (Haviland-Jones and Kahlbaugh, 2004: 303). So, if this book is resonating with you, it could just be that it reflects your own default position of who you are. With that caveat, I would still suggest that the idea of a leadership narrative is very helpful for leaders who wish to get to the heart of leadership.

Personal histories

I wanted to encourage the headteachers to reflect upon their lives and careers within a clear, but supportive framework. I started with the idea of life history, and moved, with looking at self-defining moments, or critical incidents, in to the idea of a personal leadership narrative. Life history, as Gronn and Ribbins (1996) identify, has advantages and disadvantages. Life history provides some evidence of the way that headteachers negotiate their identities and make sense of the social context. The accounts are, I hope, true to the individuals. At the same time these accounts can only ever be a portion of the truth. In a book I have only space for a few such accounts. The next chapter focuses on people and personal history, and begins to apply emotion to leadership situations in schools.

A life history can be examined for the emotional components of leadership. Stories resonate in different ways with different people:

> The story is not a measure of the objective truth of an event, but is a fine indicator of our feelings and how we wish to present them. (Fineman, 2003: 17)

As you read, you can see how these (emotional) attributes influenced their careers and the emphasis they have placed on their emotional lives. Interpreting personal stories, and seeking to understand the part they play in individuals' everyday lives in schools is difficult. When collecting such stories I tried as Cortazzi suggests to bring out the 'neglected humanity of teaching and learning and of its leadership' (2002: 200). I hope the headteachers' narratives will illuminate aspects of emotion in leadership for you. Autobiographical memory is also a device for leaders to reconstruct their past in response to questions. The headteachers in this study were from the primary and the secondary sector – 11 altogether, five men and six women. All were between the ages of 42 and 55 when interviewed. All had their leadership described by Ofsted as good or outstanding. The contexts of the schools varied from very challenging in terms of high deprivational indices to areas of less deprivation. Researching with them is how I began to frame my own thoughts about how headteachers experience emotion and meaning. Most of all it began a process for me of asking how this emotional management impacts on their approach to leadership.

Although the sample size was small, it is interesting to note that despite the very different contexts and sizes (from 150 to 367 on roll in the primary, up to 1500 in the secondary sector) their views on emotion and leadership were very similar.

Emotional experiences

All the emotional experiences that the headteachers described to me are the way that they have interpreted their own emotional state at the time. One of the values of thinking about a leadership narrative is that it makes you more aware of how your emotional state can be influenced by various situations in schools. Some emotional states you can be very aware of, some are more subconscious. For example, Eleanor told me this story:

> I had a very difficult year group with aggressive boys and children who just didn't get on. One very difficult boy had to be sent home one day. His father was a big man, who had been to prison. The child told the father that the teacher had assaulted him. He came into school, and I was terrified. He said, 'I want that teacher here NOW', and so I called the deputy and the teacher and was ready to call the police. I felt worried and frightened for the teacher and myself physically. Then the child kicked the teacher, and the father's attitude changed, when he saw what the child did. It was a roller coaster of an experience, and I was quite inexperienced as a head at the time. I suppose that fear and worry were my main emotions. Palpitating heart, shaking, although not outwardly I was later told. I felt ill afterwards. I felt OK later as the father had changed his tune, and I was able to talk it all through with the deputy. But for weeks afterwards I still got panicky feelings such as I had never experienced before.

Eleanor was faced with an unknown situation in terms of her experience as a head. Her state as far as people could see at the time was that she was in control, but as she reveals, her underlying emotional state is fear. She could only really manage some of these competing stimuli at the time, and the rest afterwards, as she suggests. As the lead professional in this situation she is aware that she needs to appear in control, however difficult this may be. This example shows that there are many emotional states you can be conscious about at the time, but others that are at a much deeper, subconscious level. Subconscious awareness can be present of course – Eleanor knew she could be in trouble. This small story does illustrate many of the emotional concepts from Chapter Two, and reminds us of the fact that emotional experiences and our own cognitive ability to process them are very closely linked together.

Telling stories

I have already used some quotations from my research in order to look more closely at the reality of the schools the heads work in, but in the next chapter I will look at them in much more detail. Stories are a way to look at emotion that removes some of the 'danger' aspect of emotion. To reveal one's own vulnerability in an accountability climate may be not only difficult, but also personally sensitive. Being asked to tell a story removes some of that danger, but risks being judged in a non-serious manner.

> We are often asked as life story researchers, 'But what is the point of storytelling?' When asked what we do with our lives, we would probably dredge up more respectable titles of researcher, psychologist, policy analyst or academic. Storyteller still smacks of the last period of primary school, still lacks seriousness in the adult world. ... Stories are more than individual tales. They are the products of complicated research relationships. They are

imbued with theory, with practice and policy implications, and with humanity. ... What is the point of storytelling? The points are in the telling of stories. (Goodley et al., 2004: 195)

In this research, the person of the headteacher was particularly important, so suitable contextualisation of their life history and career is vital in order to understand the research carried out with them, and to place the headteachers as emotional beings within the schools where they lead. Josselson and Lieblich argue:

> Through narrative, we come into contact with our participants as people engaged in the process of interpreting themselves. We work then with what is said and what is not said, within the context in which that life is lived, and the context of the interview in which words are spoken to represent that life. We then must decode, recognise, recontextualize or abstract that life in the interest of reaching a new interpretation of the raw data of experience before us. (1995: ix)

Some of these lives are introduced in the next chapter. They are outlined so that you can look at how your own life has influenced your leadership narrative. Before you read them, you may like to start your own reflection by working through some of the think points below.

Think points

1 Begin to look at your leadership narrative by writing down the key incidents, people and places that have informed you as a leader.
2 Can you identify moments in your leadership narrative, when your own sense of self was strongest or weakest? Why might this have been?

continued over

Think points *continued*

3 What do you want people to know about you as a person? How does this relate to your leadership style?

4 Oatley and Jenkins conclude that emotional events that remain clearly in the memory have the following features:

- The event must be salient and perceived as strongly emotional at the time it occurs or soon afterwards.
- Your life's subsequent course must make the event focal in recall: either a turning point, the beginning of a sequence, or instrumental in later activities.
- The event must remain relatively unique. (2003: 270)

You might like to try to relate these three points to an emotional event that you have been involved with recently. Ask yourself whether that event has any echoes in your personal history.

Further reading

Lewis, M. and Haviland-Jones, J. (eds) (2004) *Handbook of Emotions*. New York: Guilford Press.
This is a book which can help you explore aspects of memory, identity and emotion further.

Loader, D. (1997) *The Inner Principal*. London: Falmer Press.
This book illustrates the personal journey of one headteacher in Australia through the use of metaphors. It's a highly personal account.

Pascal, C. and Ribbins, P. (1998) *Understanding Primary Headteachers*. London: Cassell.
If you are in the primary sector, this book is a particular resource for you.

Southworth, G. (1995) *Looking into Primary Headship: A Research Based Interpretation*. London: Falmer.
This is an in-depth study of one primary head.

Chapter 4

The people we are

Introduction

This chapter introduces some of the headteachers I interviewed. There is not enough space to look in detail at all of the headteachers, so three will be looked at in detail – two primaries, one secondary. The others will be used as examples of particular aspects of emotion, but I hope all three are relevant to educational leaders in whatever school sector they find themselves. In each case, we discussed their own leadership narrative and how this has helped make them the people they are as headteachers. The focus was on the heart of leadership and emotion, but other areas were also explored. As you read their stories, I hope you will find areas that are helpful to your own story of leadership.

It was difficult to choose which of the heads to present in detail here. The three that are in this chapter are representative, and yet not representative of English headteachers. The number is too small for representation, but I hope that there are aspects of their stories that will resonate with you.

James: the most experienced head

The most experienced headteacher in the research, James, was several terms into his third primary headship when he became part of this research. James had been a head for 21 years in three substantive headships, plus two acting headships, all in one of the original new towns in the East of England. He is in his fifties. The school where he is currently head, has 280 children, 11 classes, 16 teachers, 25 teaching assistants (TAs) and takes children with physical disabilities. Thus, it is a hybrid between mainstream and special school, and has a hydrotherapy pool and a physiotherapy room. It has two specialist teachers as support to adapt or allow access to the curriculum. The school has children with visual impairment. When James came to the school he found that the school was more a special school than a mainstream school, and one of his aims was to turn the school back into a mainstream school and include the physically handicapped children. Previously, it was too restricting for the mainstream children. He was interviewed a year into his headship. At the point he arrived (coincidentally he assured me), all the senior management team left. The youngest member of staff at the school had been there three years but most others had been there 10 years or more. The catchment area is mixed in an established town in eastern England. The area has private rented housing and also refugee housing provided by the local authority. He noted that he loses some children to other schools in the area, from what he called 'aspiring families'. The SATs results were on a rising trend when he arrived – approximately 80 per cent science, 70 per cent English, 70 per cent maths. James was very adamant that it was part of his educational philosophy that there is more to school then the tests, and other educational activities should feature strongly in the life of any school, such as trips, productions and music.

James became a headteacher because he 'wanted to run a school my way'. He didn't want to 'become a cynical classroom teacher'. He suggested that it is a young person's job in the classroom, because it is a difficult job and there are many pressures on staff. The thing that he most enjoyed about being a headteacher is helping develop staff and children. He enjoys working in a happy, achieving school. The opportunity has arisen for him to leave schools, for example to go into industry, but he enjoys moving a school forward and, when he seriously considered leaving headship, the other options did not appeal. His personal leadership narrative was told to me over several interviews, and is outlined below.

Childhood and schooling

The only boy in his family, James's schooling began in Scotland. James can remember starting school, but is not sure of his actual age. He knows that his older sister joined him there. He describes primary school as 'happy days', and a place where he enjoyed getting involved in sport. In infant school he used to go to the older boys' playground to play football with them. He knew them from the estate, as it was the sort of place where you knew everyone. The school was quite large with 20 classes, and he remembers both formal and informal things about it. He can remember the 'tawse' and also the teachers he related to well. From Year 5 to Year 7, he represented the county at football so became a 'known' person. He took the 'qually' at 11 and didn't get into the academy where his sister went. His father was quite happy as he could have appealed to get James in, but thought that the high school would be fine, and that James would fit in better there. He continued with the sport, and then when he was 15 they moved to England, where there was a different syllabus and the grammar school would not take him. He went to the secondary modern in a large southern coastal town, and started at the beginning of the two years leading up to O levels. The school created a special class for O levels of only 20 children which was started when James arrived. Everyone else took CSEs. The grammar school took you for A levels and James says these experiences are why he has 'a thing about selection'.

James sees his family as important in his life as they 'always supported, always there'. Schools gave him mixed messages about himself. Some teachers were supportive, and he can think of particular individuals to whom he could relate. At the secondary modern, for example, there were three teachers whom he respected a great deal. At the grammar school, it was slightly different — 'the values were misplaced at times'. He recalls in particular his ex-army lower sixth teacher, who was very difficult to relate to. He enjoyed his school career, and followed his sister into teaching.

James's account retains throughout the images and the voice of Scotland where he grew up, especially in its vocabulary ('tawse', 'qually'). There is also a strong narrative of personal beliefs and values as he talks about the happiness of early childhood and the closeness of the neighbourhood in which he lived. It has a nostalgic quality to it, and contains some mixed messages about schooling. Despite the formal systems and the corporal punishment that existed in the 1960s, he is clear that primary school was a happy time, and that he perceived his primary schooling as good. This is in contrast to his experience of secondary schooling. A major emotional support for him would appear to be his sporting ability that was above average, and therefore he was valued for it in schools. This was able to sustain him when other parts of his life were not so easy. He also stresses the support of his family, but his failure to get into the higher school, and the move to England at a significant time (due to examinations) are key points in the narrative in terms of the wider context. He described 'a thing about selection', and 'the values were misplaced at times', with real passion in his voice. This passion for social justice is a connection throughout his narrative. He recalls teachers whom he could relate to, and that overall he enjoyed school, which is in conflict with some of what he says overall, perhaps because he is looking at his childhood experience through adult lenses. Thus, he stresses relationships, support, passion for social justice and values in this narrative.

After school, James went to Teacher Training College in southern England where he studied geography as his major in his Cert Ed. It was a middle school (8–12) course. He was also part of the PE group. He opted for the BEd at the end of his second year, but when he did his final teaching practice he began to feel that the academic part of the course was 'jumping through hoops', and he decided he had 'had enough of essays!'

Pre-headship

Next, he moved to a developing area of England where new schools were being built. In those days, you applied to pools of teachers, and he and his wife-to-be saw the town as an opportunity for getting a new house as they came with the post there at that time. The school he was offered in the early 70s was 'the most depressing school I had ever seen'. When he saw it, he thought, 'it's a godforsaken place, there is no way I am going to stop here for very long, right?' It was in a run-down area, and even in the days before high security it had huge fences, and signs about trespassing. It was also an old building. He came away depressed from his visit. When he started teaching there he 'got sucked into the job', and learnt a great deal from it about how not to run a school. The head spent most of the time in his office. The DH and her 'henchmen' dealt with staff and 'persecuted' children. James remembers it as horrible, and one particular turning point stands out. It was the usual practice for children to return to their classroom after singing practice unaccompanied. One day, his class did not return, so he went to look for them, and found them in the hall where they were sitting being 'glowered at' by the DH. James felt that she was taking out issues with him by picking on his class. After a year, he applied for another post, but stayed and the head gave him an extra responsibility point.

Another issue that stands out in his memory from that time is the note about his dress code. The secretary brought him a note from the head in class to say that he was not adhering to the school dress code (he was wearing a polo neck). Then, at the end of the year on the school trip, the head decided on the day to come on the trip, and turned up in a safari suit, and commented that James was a bit over-dressed. After two years and a term, he made a parallel move.

The head at the new school was new in post. Within 15 months, with new appointments, his second school became a leading school in the area. James said the school had 'a how to do it' philosophy. The atmosphere was buzzing, and looking back he thinks this is what kept him in education. It enabled him to start afresh and he gained another point. His next step, encouraged by the head, after four and a half years, was to apply for the DH of a brand new school that was being set up. Again, looking back, he feels he was a bit naïve not to look more closely at the educational philosophy of the head. He moved from a democratic school to one with no democracy, and although he stayed five years, he let the LEA know after three that he was looking for a change. He applied for another DH which he did not get. He felt the staff looked to him, and they did try to involve the head but there was slow development, and, in particular, the head did not relate to parents, did not 'listen to the clientele'. For example, the staff arranged a topic week at the end of which all parents were invited into the school. The head 'did not bother to be part of it'. It was 'impossible'. A good example of the head's inflexible approach was his decree that all boards in the school should be framed in the school's colours, which the staff felt was not always desirable. He 'would not bend'.

Then, a small headship came up (80 children, 3 classes) and the Inspector asked if he was interested. He had no training at all, but there was less need then as the LEA took a great deal of the responsibility. James felt also that he had the security of knowing connections in the area, so had a ready-made support network. While he was still a DH he had been offered a chance to leave education and move into retailing. He was 'sorely tempted' but it would have involved uncertain finances and a family move so it was decided against. He was concerned that if it wasn't successful, what would he do? In some ways he regrets it, because it would have been a change to engage with the 'real world' and he does love a challenge.

James's first teaching post is described graphically in emotional terms: 'the most depressing school I had ever seen', 'a godforsaken place', which raises the question of whether this was how he actually felt at the time, or sees it in retrospect because it was a difficult school to work in. Both perceptions may be valid, and can be related to his overall passion for social justice. The descriptions of the school when he was actually working in it are also clear and unequivocal in terms of what the school felt like as a place to work:

'Learnt a great deal from it about how *not* to run a school'
The deputy head and her 'henchmen'
'Persecuted' children
'Horrible'
Class being 'glowered at' by the deputy head
Unfair application of the dress code.

Both the headteacher and the deputy are portrayed unfavourably. This contrasts starkly with his next school, which is described as:

A leading school in the area
Has 'a how to do it' philosophy
Atmosphere was buzzing
Enabling him to start afresh.

The head, and this support, actively encouraged him to move to a deputy headship, and the atmosphere in the school, he suggests, is what kept him in education. It is interesting to note that he felt he was naïve in the choice of his next post, and that he should have looked more closely at the new head's philosophy. His telling of the next stage of his career is redolent of disappointment – 'no democracy', 'slow', head 'not bothered', 'impossible', head inflexible, 'would not bend'. He did look outside education at this stage ('the real world'), but despite having no headship training he felt that he could move on because of the security he had in knowing connections in the area, and a ready-made support network.

James's narrative style is very striking and again I would suggest that relationships (the way he talks about the people he works with), support for self (noticeable especially when he discusses career) and his passion for social justice (his emphasis on what education is fundamentally about) are key themes running through his story.

Headship

James moved into headship with no official preparation except what he had absorbed from his other schools. As he said, he had discovered how not to run a school from his experiences, and the first two sentences of what follows show that he had a clear idea of what he values in a school.

James was really looking forward to headship. He knew what he wanted to see in practice, and he knew that he wanted to put children at the centre of it all. His LEA was one of the first to take up LMS (Local Management of Schools), so he benefited from that. He loved the school, but was maybe 'too happy, too long' and after seven years found that he was being turned down for the headships of larger schools on the grounds of his inexperience in larger schools. The Assistant Director of Education suggested to him that he could gain this experience helping at a local school that was 'about to go down'. He looked after this school for two and a half terms and enjoyed the experience. Within a year of this, he had moved to a much larger school. This was a very rewarding experience, 'a great deal of happiness in the place'. Again, he was asked to help for several terms at a local school that had gone into special measures. The irony was that this was that same, depressing school in which his career had started. Following his time there, he moved to his current school, where he has been for a year.

The way that James told this to me illustrates how deeply storytelling is involved in biography. The return to the first school was said with the verve of someone revealing an exciting plot dénouement in a serial. Also, both of the schools that he enjoyed are talked about in terms of happiness – 'too happy, too long' and 'a great deal of happiness in the place'. This part of the interview engendered fresh understanding of James as a person who values support and good relationships, but as his professional confidence grows he is prepared to take risks (the schools in special measures) in order to help children have opportunities. This ties in with his view in the first interview that the thing that he most enjoys about headship is helping to develop staff and children, and working in a happy achieving school (it was clear that by this he did not mean SATs results.).

If we regard James's story as his personal leadership narrative, leadership and emotion appear to be closely linked. First, the narrative points to a direct emotional comparison between his childhood difficulties at school and his choice of headship experiences. Again, this is related to his passion for social justice. Second, these childhood difficulties, especially at secondary school, have shaped the way he approaches his own leadership in schools. The inherent and socially constructed aspects of emotion are brought into sharp focus in the way he has experienced life. The emotions and feelings that he has experienced in childhood and early teaching (or returning to Lupton's categories of emotion, it is socially constructed, but with an inherent temperament), have shaped how he views headship. So the way he practises leadership is influenced by his emotions. As James commented in the interviews, he sometimes feels he is acting, and the emotional regulation of leadership was important to him, as emotional regulation had been important through difficult times in his own schooling. At the same time, decisions he has made about his career have had an emotional weighting, and the emotional context provided by the headteachers he worked for has influenced his own views on the role of the headteacher.

Laura: the new school experience

The second most experienced headteacher in the research is Laura. We met on a headteacher training course where I was impressed by her dynamism. Laura had been a head-teacher for 12 years when she was interviewed. She is in her early fifties. Her first headship was in a two-teacher small vil-lage primary in a leafy English county, and following that she became head of a new school on a green field site in a large market town in the same county. Her current school is one of the biggest primary schools in the county. She set up this school from scratch, picked her own staff team, and was able to furnish the school and resource it with her own educa-tional philosophy in mind.

The school was built for a new estate in a town on the corridor of a major motorway. More houses were then built and Laura had to manage large expansion of the site. At first, the school was single entry, with seven classes. Year on year the school expanded and they had to have mobile class-rooms and eventually a large extension was built. There are now 18 classes, six part-time teachers, 11 TAs and a non-teaching deputy with 420 on roll. Laura makes it part of her practice 'to grow staff', and many staff are people who either started their career there, or have come back there after having a family. For example, she has a policy of never having supply teachers, which she has done for three years, and has no staff insurance scheme. She believes that investing in your staff will be repaid.

The catchment area is diverse. It has a highly mobile pop-ulation with people moving on in terms of jobs. It is an area of blue-collar work, with both parents working and high employment, but it is 'culturally deprived'. She noted, 'Children are not talked to'. There is a high amount of family break-up — almost one a week in the school. Laura suggested that it was a 'must have' society locally.

Laura originally worked in an EBD outreach for 5- to 16-year-olds, working with schools and heads. She had no headship ambitions at that stage, but wondered what she would do next. She thought of becoming an adviser, and then a head, and 'sort of fell into headship', when she applied for one. Laura's motivation for being a head revolves around the fact that she loves moving people forward, and would say that she is passionate about education and children. She feels that children have one chance at school and that it should be in a secure and loving environment. She thinks she has a good relationship with parents, and has always put an emphasis on developing adults in schools as well as children.

Laura actually enjoys most things in headship, even the difficult things. She enjoys being a facilitator. Things that can be wearing are factions, usually due to personality, she believes; 'Troublesome people can be tiring!' She enjoys the reading and writing part of the job, and finds it a useful intellectual challenge, even keeping paperwork in order.

Childhood and schooling

Laura's early childhood was that of an only child at home with her parents and maternal grandmother. She could read before she went to school, and remembers herself at this period as a 'savage', roaming the woodlands near her house, and playing out with the local boys. Her most significant memory of starting school is that her brother was born at the same time, or just before she went to school, and she recalls him arriving with no explanation at all, or anything in the way of preparation. At around about the same time, she had to have her tonsils removed, and remembers the nurse in hospital slapping her. The cruelty of that incident remains strong in her memory. She went to a church primary school, which was not the one that the majority of her friends went to, and she recalls this as lonely and isolating, coming to grips with 'strange new rules'. She didn't enjoy school as she found the books boring and it all rather confusing. At seven the school became all girls, and she recalls it as very high church, involving a lot of church services. She quite enjoyed the pageantry aspect of it, the incense and the Latin. She recalls Miss Smith in the lower juniors as being very sympathetic. She also remembers that they seemed hardly ever to do PE, and she remembers making a hippo out of clay. The top class was in rows according to your academic performance leading up to the 11-plus, and the teacher drank. It was very competitive. She passed the 11-plus and went to the girls' grammar school and she is 'not girly!' It was in a beautiful place, and she went by coach. She felt a sense of dislocation at school, and somehow different as she was from a working class background – the girls were asked to state their father's profession on the first day. She strongly believes that your philosophy of education comes from childhood, and although she enjoyed the work and most of the teachers at the grammar school, she does not think it is a good system.

In contrast to James's settled picture of his family context as a child, Laura talks about her childhood in terms of struggle and dislocation – wildness, loss, strangeness, but also of beauty. She talks of herself as wild and roaming, a bit of a tomboy. It is very illuminating that the stories of her brother's birth and the hospital are juxtaposed, perhaps because of their close connection in time, or because of their similarity in terms of emotional recall. Both were unexpected and harsh events in her life. Whether or not they were actually close together does not matter, as emotionally they are strongly connected for her.

She tells vividly of the strangeness of primary school for the young child – 'lonely', 'isolating' are the words she uses. The strangeness was also positive in terms of pageantry – the incense and the Latin of the church services. Also, she contrasts the two teachers that she remembers most, one fondly, and one 'who drank'. In her description of secondary school, she reiterates the tomboy, 'not girly', and her strong feelings about the class system where girls had to 'state their father's profession on the first day'.

Values and a passion for social justice/fairness are important childhood themes for Laura, but so are feelings and a sense of otherness. Gender also features strongly. Of all the interviewees, she was the one who told her story in the most dramatic fashion.

Post-school

Laura had no real idea what she wanted to do with her life, although she considered, she told me, various quite exotic options such as spy or archaeologist. She did RE, English and history at A level, although university was not really part of her family's experience and she heard friends talking about teaching so she began to look at prospectuses. She knew that she wanted to work with people, and rather liked the look of one of the teacher training colleges – Edmonds Hall, because of its location in the country but near a city. She also had a very positive teacher role model, which may have influenced her decision.

Her college course was for 5–7 infants, and she found it 'surprisingly interesting!' She studied RE and design as her subject options, and did a Cert Ed. She didn't want to stay on and do a BEd as she was fed up with studying and schools. By then she had also met her first husband. She credits him with broadening her horizons.

The way this is told seems to suggest that she fell into teaching ('surprisingly interesting!'), although friends and teacher role models obviously played a part. The half-joking/half-serious way she mentioned exotic occupations for me expressed her personality – able to 'bubble', but be serious at the same time. Like James, she felt that she had come to the end of study. The description she provides is of a person in transition from school to something new and exciting.

Pre-headship

I have divided her pre-headship experience into two parts, because of the career break in the middle, and the move to a special unit. Laura's 'patchwork' career pattern (which is replicated in other married women headteachers that I interviewed), is a feature of women's career patterns more generally, in that their working lives can be influenced by the work patterns of partners (Hall, 1996).

Laura applied to work in a large English shire county. She was sent to work in a junior school in a market town, which was very large – there were 600 in the infants, plus 600 in the juniors and many of the children had been relocated from Birmingham and London, so they were not easy. It was run by a Yorkshire head with 'a rod of iron', who was very particular and did things 'in a certain way'. It was very much strong leadership, but she also remembers lots of artwork and residentials. He was also 'flawed' and he smoked and drank, which made him 'more human'. She recalls the excellent inset in the teaching of art. The staff were young with an average age of 28, with an equal number of male and female teachers. She said 'it was the best start you could have had – strict but caring'. She stayed for three years, and then they had a largish pay award so she and her husband decided to resign and go see the world. They were away for 9–10 months visiting Europe, Turkey, Iran, Afghanistan, India, Nepal and Ceylon. It was 'a life-changing experience'. When she returned, she went into schools and did some supply work. Then she got a job in a three-teacher school, which had a very different way of working to her first school – it was all themed and planned, and the head was a full-time teacher. It had close links with the community. She met her second husband. She felt that both her schools gave her formative experiences in which she learnt about how children learn. She was there for two and a half years, and left to have her first son. She had three children in close succession, and did some odd supply days, then went back full-time after eight years.

Laura's telling of her early career is punctuated by the

occurrence of personal events: travel and pregnancy, unlike that of James. Like him, however, she is conscious of the impact of the headteacher on a school. She draws a dramatic picture of a man who is very particular, does things in a certain way, rules with a rod of iron, drinks and smokes. Interestingly, she regards these flaws as positives as they made him 'more human'. This is summed up by the phrase that she uses: 'it was the best start you could have had – strict but caring'.

While bringing up her children, Laura had done some supply work with children with statements and a vacancy came up at the Support Unit. She felt that she had had enough of class teaching and liked the relationships you could forge with children in the unit. It was more interesting. She worked with 5–18-year-olds and advised schools and heads and children who came to the unit. She also did a lot of work with families which she enjoyed. Her first head was very charismatic and positive; very clear and caring, and she views him as another role model. He left and his replacement she describes as 'passive/aggressive' and a chain smoker. He was also very disorganised. She learnt a great deal about behaviour management at the unit, especially 'about how you have to be'. She discovered that 'management was being about people wanting to be managed by you'. She also at this time did a two-year counselling course and a psychodrama course. After the counselling course, she also embarked on a Master's degree which was a significant turning point in terms of confidence in her intellectual and organisational ability. By this time, she had worked with many heads and was not impressed with some of them. She didn't want to become a deputy under a head that she didn't feel was competent so was in a dilemma. A way out came from the LEA, who suggested a village headship in a difficult area (three children out of the 50 had statements for behaviour management).

When she looks back at the heads she has worked with, she feels that Trevor (the first) had authority and a vision of what the school should be like. The second, Daniel, was also visionary and sure of the importance of art and drama, and the links with self-esteem. He had a brilliant sense of humour as well as love of children which meant that the school was full of laughter. This is something Laura also wanted (and felt she partially achieved) in her own school. He also showed her the importance of links with parents. Martin showed her that 'children love zap'. He was an attractive figure. By the way he didn't behave, Douglas showed her how important it is to look after staff and recognise their needs.

Laura's feelings about the headteachers she worked with come out extremely strongly here. They are clearly people who she looked to for leadership. Positive aspects include: charismatic and positive; very clear and caring; authority; visionary; attractive; links with self-esteem. Negatives are noted ('passive/aggressive') but turned into positives by the way that Laura views the way they affected her (by the way he didn't behave). There is a clear thread of performance and optimism running through all this. This can be seen by phrases such as: 'children love zap' and 'about how you have to be'. She also enjoyed having her three sons and being a mother at home. She also credited her husband with being a brilliant and inspirational teacher, who also became a head-teacher and throughout her career pushed and encouraged her – 'he always recognised what I could do and made me feel that I could achieve anything I wanted. Note the push as well as encourage! I don't think I would have had the confidence to do a lot of this without him'. The themes that run throughout her leadership narrative are values, support for staff and self, gender, performance and optimism.

Summary

Both James and Laura are primary headteachers with a considerable amount of experience between them. At the heart of their leadership are strong values that they have developed throughout their lives, and which have proved important to them in such aspects of their career as job choice. They are very different people in terms of personality, but there are similarities in their leadership narrative. For example, both of them were influenced by leaders who dealt with people in ways that Laura and James felt was not appropriate for a headteacher – 'By the way he didn't behave Douglas showed her how important it is to look after staff and recognise their needs'. Many of the incidents they describe will also be familiar, emotionally, to secondary school leaders. I have chosen to present a male secondary head because gender stereotyping might suggest that a man in such a leadership position would not find the idea of a leadership narrative and emotion useful. This did not prove to be the case.

Tim: a secondary head

Tim was a secondary headteacher, several years into his first headship when interviewed. His school was in a challenging area, and was slightly smaller than the average secondary school (just over 800 pupils), with over a hundred staff in all categories. Tim felt that the school was a type that he wanted to work in as one of his main aims as a headteacher was to make a difference in children's lives. Underlying values are again very important to this leader.

The school was on an established but socially deprived estate in England. It has suffered from declining roles and not being seen for several years as the school of choice for parents in the area. Tim suggested that aspirations for the children were not set high enough when he arrived, partly because 'the school had not got into tune fully with the national raising attainment agenda that existed – it was, possibly, still too focused on its caring and pastoral responsibility – a function it fulfilled very well and still does.' He saw the challenge of removing 'the glass ceiling to achievement that existed all around' in students, some staff, the parents/carers. This low aspiration seemed entrenched in many, for example, an aspiration would be 'she wants to be a hairdresser'. He was also aware of the emotional history of the school in terms of local tensions and what he called, 'bureaucracy — targets with no relevance to real agenda on the ground'

The catchment area is similar to Laura's with a highly mobile population with people moving on, but often because of housing relocation by the council or first stop for asylum seekers rather than jobs (25 per cent movement over a four-year period). It is not an area of high unemployment but many low-paid jobs. All the schools in the area, primary and secondary, have struggled over the last 10 years to deal with being in one of the most deprived boroughs in England, and school results which often do not achieve government minimum standards. Leading the school, Tim suggested, was 'a real battle initially, and having the courage to make the hard, right decisions, and not to duck the challenge is part of being a head'. He also noted that he saw part of his role to be involved in the wider community in the fullest sense, and to be never satisfied with what is there already. He described himself as, 'the eternal optimist — glass always half full'. Given my work on primary schools in challenging circumstances and the emotion involved, Tim seemed a very interesting headteacher to talk with.

Tim went into teaching with a desire 'to make things better', and described how he wanted to harness 'young people's energy and their capacity for betterment'. He entered teaching in the late 1970s when it was difficult for newly qualified teachers to get posts, and at that point he did not feel up to a big inner-city challenge. He enjoys headship with what he calls, ' a kind of arrogance, wanting to be a good boss and a role model as a leader to everybody associated with the school'.

Childhood and schooling

Tim went to one infant/junior school and had a stable family background with one younger sister. He then moved to a boys' grammar school which was very academic, but it also had a strong sports ethos, and valued sport as a way of moving forward with your life. As a pupil, he said that he was never 'an outright rogue, but got into plenty of trouble. Studying did not compete easily against sport. I got better at learning and achievement as I got older!' Tim became heavily involved with team sports, football, rugby, cricket, hockey etc., at school and county level. His father was very well read and pro education, as he felt he had never had a chance in his own occupation to use his knowledge, because he felt trapped in his job. Tim's mother was a school cook, and he was the first person at university in his family. He recalls the beginning of his sports university course as alerting him even more strongly to what he was doing when he heard a lecture whose theme was 'What are you here for?' He suggested that this is when he began to be really aware of his own inner drive to teach, which he had not considered before.

Tim's values and a passion for social justice/fairness are even more explicit in the telling than Laura's, and he spoke of these with a particular passion. Family also features strongly. His uncle was a founding trade unionist when it was not easy to be supporting workers' rights. Tim's story is told with a focus on how the past reflects where he is now.

Pre-headship

After university Tim married, and found himself (as did many other teachers in the late 1970s) in the position of really having to hunt for a post. He made more than 20 applications to many different types of schools before finding his first post in a deprived area outside London. At that time, he told me, he had no idea of what real deprivation was, or how policy might influence schools. He realised after about 18 months that this was the kind of secondary school in which he wanted to work as a PE teacher. He then became, as he put it, 'gripped by English', and PE became secondary.

After four years he moved to another school in the Thames corridor to become second in department, and acting head of department. He became head of creative arts, and he found that this school was more middle class with different pressures on teachers. Tim said that he felt 'like a fish out of water' in the school. Eventually, via the TVEI initiative, he became acting deputy, which quickly became substantive. It was a good career move, as he learnt all about curriculum and timetabling – 'I passionately believe the answer to most school problems lies in curriculum structure, pedagogy in the classroom and through their administration tool which is the timetable. Flexibility and courage are the key drivers in planning, not easy in a very regulated National Curriculum that was'. But he felt he began to get stuck and question some of the policy initiatives that the school was involved with – going grant maintained, for example. At the same time he did a part-time Master's in educational management, focusing on SEN and student exclusion. He applied for the headship at the school but did not get it. The new head was good to work with and he stayed for another three years.

Tim began to apply for other headships and he put in several applications and had many unsuccessful interviews in a variety of secondary schools all over the country. He tried for headships on and off for several years without success and felt he would have benefited from some coaching and understanding earlier to realise the difference between the two days of interview. He had passed the NPQH in the first cohort (1998). By now, he had been a deputy for 11 years and felt he was very ready for a move. Finally, he decided to make another effort, bought the TES and made five applications in a week. He had two interviews – one still in the Thames corridor, and the other miles away. He got the latter which was the first interview sequentially. When he reflects back on his headship interviews he believes the thing that attracted his current school – his tendency to 'wear his heart on his sleeve' – was not well thought of by other secondary interview panels. It may, he thinks, have frightened some of them. He suggests that at his current school governors saw that he was someone that you could trust the school with.

It is a school in challenging circumstances, but is a job that he 'loves passionately'. It is an intense job, and Tim feels that, as someone who is quite an emotional person, he needs to 'never cry at work' and be able to switch from being quite 'hard' to his natural self as required. When he is angry, he aims for controlled anger as it can be good 'for people to see that you are angry occasionally'. He tries to direct passion, he says, at unfairness and likes the school to be seen as part of the solution not part of the problem. He likes a challenge, change and the intensity of the job. His aim as a head is to have a school that is 'corporate and collective', with flat leadership structures and the creative energy that comes from exchanging ideas at all levels. As he said, 'the more people that hold the school's emotional values the better for the students and community we serve.'

Tim's leadership narrative clearly sees himself as someone who has clear professional values and almost a mission to work with challenging schools. Again, as with Laura, there is a thread of performance and optimism running through all this. Tim's optimism in the face of challenges comes over even more strongly. There could be some relation in leadership narratives between this quality and the extent of the challenges for leadership. Passion for the job comes across from Tim. This can be seen by phrases such as: 'hearts and minds' and 'what I've been appointed to do'. The emotional themes that run throughout his leadership narrative are again about values, the performance part of headship, and the relevance, or otherwise, of emotional displays.

Chapter 5

The people we work with

Introduction

I have already argued how knowledge of emotion and leadership is one of the keys to the management of people in schools. This chapter emphasises the importance of the social side of emotion, and reminds us that the social context of any particular school has deep connections with your own personal leadership narrative. Both the emotional context of the school, and difficult emotions will be looked at in more depth.

Emotions as socially constructed

When working with headteachers, it is the social construction of emotion that usually provokes most discussion. If your view is that emotions are primarily socially constructed, this has obvious applications to schools, and those who lead within them. From the social perspective, defining emotion is very dependent on a person's own judgement of a situation. Norman Denzin suggested that, 'People are their emotions. To understand who a person is, it is necessary to understand emotion' (1984: 1). There are difficulties inherent in understanding an individual's inner experience, which you may like to explore in the further reading. In terms of getting to the heart of leadership, I am going to suggest that it is the way in which a person processes real and imagined social relationships that is important for the leader to understand. A way of understanding this viewpoint is the old adage 'Perception is reality', which you may have come across on various leadership courses. The three heads I introduced you to in the last chapter all had their own particular ways of looking at the social world. Each person in a school experiences that social world in various ways. How schools are experienced by staff, pupils and parents (the people we work with), may seem to be the same, but often are radically different for different individuals and groups. These perceptions will vary more widely as the size of the school increases. Teachers may acknowledge the effects, for example, of a child moving into a larger school, but adults often fail to realise that the same is true for them, especially in terms of emotional demands upon them. Staff relationships can become more complex and harder to manage, and this chapter will look at aspects of this.

In Chapter One, I made a distinction between emotion, feelings and moods. Another idea that educational leaders should be able to distinguish as a useful idea is that of *emotionality*. This is the actual process of being emotional, when the self is involved in day-to-day activities. The idea comes from the work of Norman Denzin, and more details are given at the end of the chapter if you wish to explore this further. Emotionality is not only about how you are feeling in any situation, but also how you position feelings that you direct or feel towards others. In any given situation a leader will have to position themselves emotionally in the face of others' accounts of situations. This may be with staff, parents or students. These emotional accounts link to the idea of a leadership narrative because you will be influenced by the past, however unknowingly. An area that particularly affects how we work with others is that of difficult emotions.

Difficult emotions

Although the concept of emotions as socially constructed is very helpful to leaders in schools, it is not the only approach that has value. Oatley and Jenkins (2003) suggest that the key contribution of a psychodynamic approach to the study of emotion is to demonstrate that emotions are not simple and clear-cut. Often the meanings of emotion only become clear when they are expressed outwardly, either to another or by further reflections or psychoanalysis. The psycho-dynamic approach to emotion can be particularly useful in regard to emotions that are deemed 'difficult'. Emotions of all kinds can move from the unconscious level of the mind to the conscious, influencing motivation and action in social situations. Staff in schools can use much of their energy coping with feelings that have the potential to cause harm or disruption, such as hate, fear, etc. For leaders, this aspect of emotion has the power to change the working context significantly. At the end of the chapter you will find further readings that explore this in more detail. Some might argue that the study of the relationship of the conscious to the unconscious could be seen as limited in its practical impli-cations. How can you ever really know as a leader what other people are feeling? Despite this caveat, awareness of this aspect of unconscious feeling is important for a head-teacher, especially when they are looking at how the people in the school work together.

How do people deal with difficult problems in school? James suggests that psychodynamic theory can help uncover and explain organisational processes. Faced with such problems that involve difficult feelings, James argues that, as a social defence, most people split off their difficult feelings and project them upon someone or something else (James, 2003; see also James and Jones, 2003). James suggests that this is how many teachers and leaders in education cope with genuine emotional difficulty – by other people becoming the 'good' or the 'bad' object. For example, in the case of negative emotion, the head might suggest that the real problem at the school is not the pupils; it is the paperwork/the parents/the local authority. Of these difficult emotions, shame, embarrassment and anxiety are central to the psychodynamic perspective of organisations. These specific emotions touch on our own feelings and how we deal with others. People do not like to feel anxious or embarrassed. They set up social defence mechanisms to protect themselves from these difficult feelings. In schools, leaders could cope with a difficult emotion such as shame by passing it down the organisation. For example, with a comment like 'it was not me as the head of year who forgot to get that important document signed, it was your problem for not reminding me in time'. This predisposition is an emotional avoidance strategy by the leader as it avoids having to deal with their own strong emotion. This is also an example of splitting or projecting emotion elsewhere. Lupton suggests that, 'Individuals within groups can project destructive feelings such as anxiety and fear, so that the group takes on these' (1998: 29). This was something that I noticed in schools in special measures, and was noted by Richardson in her study of a secondary school in the early seventies:

> The study of the management structures in the expanding schools of today takes little account of the extent to which unrecognised and largely unconscious feelings that teachers have about each other and about their pupils may be hindering the conscious, rational efforts being

> made by those same teachers, as professional persons, to implement desirable changes in their system. (1973: 11)

Richardson's perspective on secondary schools was hugely influenced by the psychoanalytic approach to organisations. She argued that a headteacher, particularly in a large secondary school, is pivotal emotionally because s/he is the emotional buffer between the school staff and the community of the school more generally. The important leadership skills needed, she thought, were to do with being able as a head to work with groups of staff in school and community representatives. This enabling function of the head's leadership that she suggests has links with the current vogue for distributed leadership. Most of all, however, Richardson draws our attention to the uncomfortable and the difficult as being so important that we ignore them to the disservice of education.

More recently in the leadership field, Gronn's writings (Gronn, 2003; see also Gronn and Lacey, 2004) acknowledge the power of workplace emotion in relation to leadership, and trace the way that this has evolved over time. In particular, Gronn notes that the balance between the rational and emotional aspects of leadership has changed over the years, often in response to national policies, which require task-orientated or person-orientated leadership (Gronn, 2003: 130). He also observes that there has been more or less work into the rise and fall of heart work or head work depending on national policy ideologies (Gronn referring to Barley and Kunda, 1992). At some stage in their relations with their followers and colleagues, all educational leaders (male or female) can become psychological containers for other people's emotions (Gronn, 2003: 131). In particular this highlights the vulnerability of headteachers under the thrust towards accountability, as I noted in Chapter One.

Holding the fort?

It would seem then that the holding or containing role is an important one for the headteacher, but managing anxiety within the school serves to emphasise the headteacher's own personal vulnerability. How the headteacher manages these potentially toxic emotions (Frost and Robinson, 1999) is crucial not only to the success of his/her leadership but also to their own personal well-being. The concept of the 'wounded leader', drawn by Ackerman and Maslin-Ostrowski (2004), illustrates this. This research looked at how leaders managed what they call 'the chronic conditions of leadership life: vulnerability, isolation, fear and power' (2004: 311). After hearing the stories of many leaders in North America, Ackerman and Maslin-Ostrowski conclude:

> After listening to many leader stories, we make the assumption that the interpersonal and intrapersonal experience of leadership wounding is itself a defining characteristic of leaders, an important source of emotional and social learning and a critical opening to the exercise of leadership. (2004: 313)

If wounding is a defining characteristic of leaders, particularly in the way that it helps them learn more about themselves as leaders, then it would seem correct to argue that this experience is essential, and cannot be rationalised out of the leaders' experiences. This serves to highlight the fact not only of the importance of emotion in leadership for sustainability, but also draws our attention to the aspects of emotion and leadership that have a wounding impact on leaders' lives.

Why follow the leader?

I want to return again to Richardson's *The Teacher, the School, and the Task of Management* (1973). It is a seminal book in the history of educational leadership and management, and yet not very well known today. It is one of the suggested readings for this chapter, but is worth sketching out here too. Her work is almost unique in its complete, long-term view of an educational organisation and its component parts. For three years in the late 1960s and early 1970s, Richardson worked in Nailsea Secondary School near Bristol. She was perhaps one of the first people in the educational management field to refer implicitly to emotion in the study of leadership and relationships by her focus on staff relationships.

Richardson suggests that every member of a school – whether pupil or teacher – needs to feel that he or she belongs to at least one *sentient group*, or a group of people working together who are able to respond to each other emotionally as well as intellectually.

> It is from this sentient group that we draw the emotional strength that enables us to do our jobs. If there were no satisfaction in belonging to such groups we should be personally weakened and therefore less effective in our roles. Sentient groups are not necessarily related to tasks, but in a healthy institution they ought to be. (1973: 23)

Sentient groups are about belonging, and personal relationships. They may be related to parts of the school in terms of subject areas, for example 'the science group'. They may be related to activities that go on outside of school, for example the area headteachers' network may be a sentient group. Sentient groups are about *feelings of belonging* rather than ways of behaving in a particular group. Such feelings of belonging may well be stronger in a small primary school. The boundaries between the work group and the personal in the primary school are more fluid, and staff numbers smaller, making sentient groups more common and obvious to observers. The primary headteacher is often more visible to many parts of the school community from staff to parents and governors. Richardson did not regard sentient groups as cosy places. She felt that the real strength of a sentient group was that it 'has the capacity to face up to its own internal conflicts in the interests of the tasks that it has to perform' (ibid.: 36). Richardson was primarily interested in the interplay between the person and the group, and how leaders need to understand where emotion and 'rational' parts of the school merge. In particular, her work gives some good examples of why people give authority to leaders and actually follow them. Feelings of belonging are a strong part of this. She also stressed that leaders need to be able to look much more closely at those elusive unconscious mechanisms, both formal and informal, that we use when organisational life gets difficult. Knowing about projection of emotion, and the containing and enabling part of leadership is a step towards this. As Richardson puts it, quoting group relationship theorists Miller and Rice:

> an individual has no meaning except in relationship with others with whom he interacts. He uses them and they use him to express views, take action, and play roles. The individual is a creature of the group, the group of the individual. (1973: 36)

Schein (1985) also regards emotion as an important part of leadership in organisations, and as part of what makes an individual respond to a leader's authority. Unscrupulous leaders can exploit social emotions, such as fear and shame, for their own power agendas.

Schools, it has been suggested (Carlyle and Woods, 2002: 154), make use of individual and collective emotion in several important ways;

- as a bonding agent, emphasising and strengthening the relationships between people in teams

- as a means of effective communication by helping to provide the most favourable atmosphere for communication to occur
- as a way to focus in on areas of the school for quality improvement.

Richardson made clear that the interplay between emotional and rational is subtle. The leader's understanding of the emotional aspect of the school can be central not only to planning, but also to managing difficult interpersonal situations. This is a crucial part of the emotional context of leadership in schools.

Emotional context in practice: some examples from the case studies

The intensity of the role of headteacher is not in doubt. Where it is particularly apparent is when heads gave me examples of their own dealings with other people. Tim, a secondary head, talked of 'The intensity of the job – wanting to be corporate and collective' and 'winning hearts and minds'. Another secondary head, Mike, spoke of 'Leadership being all about responding to other people's feelings and situations'. Francesca, in a junior school, was very aware of the changing and developmental nature of her own strategies:

> I'm not good at allowing my own more negative emotions out! I am good at spotting others' feelings and doing something about it. If I'm upset or angry I'm not very good at sharing. It is important to control emotion in a lot of situations, certainly to do with work, and to develop a way of doing this — eyes and teeth! [She made a very funny face showing the putting on of a smile.]

This conscious putting on of a face or role, as described above by Francesca, was also a feature of the other head-teachers' viewpoints. Although I did not suggest the idea of acting to the headteachers, it often occurred spontaneously. As James, the most experienced head, put it:

> There's a great deal of acting in headship. [For example when I was at the school he had to reprimand a small boy for kicking a door; he called this 'acting cross'.] Having said that I don't often have to put on a happy face and I don't lose my temper in school. When things go wrong, the best way forward is to look at how you can stop it happening again.

James did not view 'acting cross' as an appropriate way of dealing with the emotions of adults in the school, hence the comment above about looking forward. He continued:

> I have learnt over the years not to jump in but to listen to the other side. It's human nature to be concerned over something that has gone wrong but I feel it is much better to concentrate on how to make it not happen the next time. I also think that you need to make a greater effort in school to say when things are good, not always to look at mistakes.

This was spoken in light of three very successful headships in very different contexts as a way of managing people that had worked well for him. This emotional context and the coherence between the leader and those they work with stands out clearly.

The importance of the context of schools to the effective-ness or otherwise of the leadership of the headteacher is noted in the leadership literature (Duke, 1998; Fiedler, 1978), but this emotional coherence is a fundamental key to life lived in groups. Clear understanding of the emotional context, I would argue, makes the headteacher more effec-tive as a people manager – a key part of leadership. This reflects the work of Richardson, discussed above.

The emotional context may be at the heart of why some leaders with a huge track record of success in schools fail in another context. In some schools, the task of leadership is difficult, or even impossible due to the lack of coherence in the lives of other members of the school group. This could be staff, students or parents who are continually dealing with difficult emotions. This may be due to social factors, such as poverty and deprivation, but it can also be subtler, and go back into the school's leadership history. Emotional context is powerful when it is positive:

> I think that the closer the staff become, the less I have to deal with the fringe issues, as things begin to just happen. (James)

If a group is close, the contextual power of emotion will inspire such emotions as confidence, enthusiasm and trust (Kemper, 2004). Similarly, Ben, the newly appointed head talked about openness and how you can tell that things are beginning to cohere:

> Partly it is about perception of where the school is going, and sharing in it. Ideally you want everybody to be pulling in the same direction, involvement, the chipping in of ideas and this involves commitment, emotionally.

Emotional commitment to ideas is important for leadership, as is emotional understanding of the school community more generally. Several of the headteachers talked about the complete emotional context of the school, that is, not just within the school's physical boundaries, but the school community as a whole:

> It's creating a climate … difficult parents know that they'll be listened to, if not agreed with. (Eleanor)

> On a basic level, it is that you can see that the whole community knows that you care about the whole school and then even more at a more detailed level about specific people (mum in hospital, etc.). These are the things that are important and delightful. (Francesca)

'Important and delightful' encapsulated Francesca's idea of what emotional context in the school was about, which was part of her underlying values of an ethic of care for individuals. As she put it:

> I try to encourage caring as a staff as it is good for individual self-esteem and teams. I always send each child a Christmas card.

Mary encapsulated some of the difficulty of the emotional context because it suggests how an experienced head makes use of the emotional textures of leadership:

> I can have fierce conversations with parents or staff, but I think it is appropriate to let people know why you are feeling as you are, try and get them to see how their behaviour contributed to the situation, and to move on from it.

This emotional context will influence how a headteacher will have to regulate his or her emotions in response to situations. If the staff works closely (emotionally) together (as Ben and James suggest above), the head may be more able to have 'fierce conversations'. Similarly, context will also have a large bearing on whether a headteacher feels secure in terms of emotion-weighted decision-making.

One could argue that it is the striving of the headteacher towards emotional coherence in leadership that is important, as it seems most influential on the emotional context. Coherence may not be possible without a headteacher who is able 'to be a headteacher', in other words, someone who can play the role and regulate their own emotions sufficiently to influence others. This apparently simple statement belies not only the emotional labour involved, but also the personal background of the headteacher. To finish this chapter I would like to use one of the heads as an example of this. As you read it, see if you can relate the idea of emotional textures to the story that I put together from our interview.

Gill: experienced headteacher

Gill was an experienced headteacher of a medium sized (200 pupils) Church of England junior school in a market town in the west of England. The school was her third headship in the church section of education, and she had been in post for just over 18 months when I talked to her. I knew her from a training course that I had led, where she had been vocal in her opinions about current difficulties in primary schools due to staff shortages. I interviewed her at a time of great personal tension when it had become obvious that her school was to close in a local merger with the infant school to become an all-through primary school. She had decided to apply for the new headship, but expressed the view that she would not be the favoured candidate as the infant head was 'better liked' by the governors, and would get the post. This in fact turned out to be the case, and Gill later took early retirement. It should be noted too, that the interview itself was carried out under difficult circumstances. Staff and children with queries constantly interrupted us. There was also tension in the school that day because one of the younger pupils had been the victim of an attempted abduction by a non-custodial parent the day before. However, Gill was very forthcoming about why she had gone into headship – it seemed to be the expected thing in teaching to do that. She enjoyed being a head because she valued 'seeing plans come to fruition with children,' but found that tasks such as having to deal with staff redundancies alongside the merger 'ripped me apart'. The word she used to describe what emotion meant to her seemed to reflect the

> difficult situation she found herself in: 'tense, angry, over-whelmed, astonished' were the words that came to her mind when I asked about what emotions she could name. She told me of the situation regarding the merger, and the governors meeting that dealt with how staff would have to be made redundant, and that she would have to apply for the merger headship. She felt that it had been made very clear that her job was to 'clear up' the staff before the merger, but that there would be no place for her afterwards. The language she used to describe her feelings as she came out of this meeting was very evocative: 'I was wearing a beige jacket, and when I came out my skin was the same colour as the jacket! [...] I was wrung out like a wilted lettuce'.

Gill was in a very obviously emotional state due to school plus family difficulties at the time I was talking to her. She illustrates how someone who was previously successful at the tasks of headship was struggling with the emotional context of the merger, staff emotions, and family problems that she could not ignore. In effect, she was being asked to put these aside and deal rationally with the merger issues ('clear up the staff'), without any acknowledgement of the emotional toll this was taking on her. Due to all that was happening, I didn't feel it appropriate to carry out some of the more emotionally taxing parts of the research, and she dropped out of the study. I am including her here, at the conclusion to this chapter, for two reasons. One is to illustrate the power of the emotional context. The other is to ask whether schools sometimes ask too much of their leaders, ethically and personally. I will return to this thought in Chapter Seven.

The people we work with emotionally are the context of the school. The places we work can also influence our own leadership narrative, and give us moments of both great emotional power and weakness. The next chapter looks at some of these in the lives of the heads in the study.

Think points

1 Looking back over the book so far, which three ideas have you found most useful so far and why?

2 Can you identify the sentient group you belong to in school? Is it as important as Richardson suggests?

3 Describe your current organisation's emotional context. What are the most important aspects for the leader to understand and why?

4 Write down a critical incident that involved a difficult emotion. What emotions did you show at the time? What are your thoughts about it now? Return to this after you have read the next chapter.

5 Having read the story of Gill you have probably formed a picture of the situation in your own mind. Examine your emotional response to her story.

6 What is the most important aspect of emotion and leadership to you?

Further reading

Denzin, N. (1984) *On Understanding Emotion*. San Francisco: Jossey-Bass.
I found this book very useful in understanding the intensity of emotion and how it relates to our own personal context.

Harris, B. (2007) *Supporting the Emotional Work of School Leaders*. London: Sage.
This book will help you explore the psychological aspects of emotion and schools in more depth.

Layard, R. (2005) *Happiness: Lessons from a New Science*. London: Penguin.
This influential book relates the current work that is being

carried out into how influential happiness can be as a concept to our overall well-being.

Richardson, E. (1973) *The Teacher, the School and the Task of Management*. London: Heinemann.
Mentioned in this chapter, and probably out of print, but if you can get hold of a copy this is an underrated classic. It focuses on a long-term study of a secondary school in Bristol. Although dated in many aspects, from the point of view of emotion and leadership, I think it still has a great deal to say.

Chapter 6

The places we work

Introduction

This chapter looks at some examples of the pivotal emotional events in headteachers' stories. Each narrative was picked because it had an emotional significance to that headteacher. I'll look at the different types of social emotion that the stories illustrate, and ask you to reflect on your own leadership narrative. The impact of emotional context will be looked at, reflecting practice and theory.

Central to the work of Richardson that was discussed in Chapter Five is the concept of organisations. Sometimes, the discussion of leadership can seem to take place without such a context, but she and other writers (Glatter, 2006) also note that the organisation must be taken into account especially when dealing with personal relationships.

The background

I invited the headteachers to talk to me about events in their professional workplace that had caused them to remember it as an emotional event, either at the time or in retrospect. This elicited various experiences with a strong emotional bias. Some of the stories also uncovered Denzin's personal epiphanies (interactional moments and experiences that leave their marks on peoples' lives), such as Ben's experience as a child (see pp. 111–118). Most of the stories were concerning negative emotional events. This is probably because of the impact of such events upon their practice.

The story of Mary's difficult teacher (which you may have already read, p. 27), was one of these – both underscore the heads' intention of giving the appearance of rationality even under some very difficult emotional pressure, and link both to emotional regulation in leadership and to emotion-weighted decision-making.

Eleanor's incidents are revealing for the aspects of emotion that can be seen within them. You have already read her encounter with the difficult parent (p. 47). They show the inherent (how she reacted internally: 'upsetting', 'uncomfortable', 'terrified', 'worried and frightened physically') and the socially constructed (the aftermath within the school which she had to deal with, difficult people). Her other event was similar in some ways:

> Earlier this year the school administrator made a written formal complaint to me about the caretaker. I had to see the caretaker and I found it upsetting as I sort of felt it was in some ways a complaint about me. I knew that the interview with the caretaker would be difficult, and in fact he stormed out! I just had to deal with it. Later he did apologise, but it left a … nasty taste. There's still an aftermath of the incident within the school – the governors sorted it by giving the caretaker a verbal warning. It was an uncomfortable feeling and I was only able to share it with the chair of governors and my husband. Who else is there? It's difficult to get hold of other heads during the day.

Such incidents also highlight other facets of leading and emotion. The interview with the 'difficult' parent was unique as it was the first time she had to deal with an incident involving such emotion. The second is memorable because she told me that in her view the most difficult issues in school are to do with managing adults. Looking back, she would have been more forceful in the first one, but was new and not confident of her knowledge of the teacher. In the second one, too, she might have been more forceful with the complainant, or as she phrased it – 'Heading things off at the pass'. Eleanor said that she had learnt that it is really important to keep a calm front (emotional regulation), and use a measured tone, especially with parents. The look on your face is important, she suggested, or as she put it: 'Must make sure you are not leaking!' This is a clear example of emotional labour in headship, and emphasises the physical side of emotion as well.

Another story that illustrates a different aspect to consider when getting to the heart of leadership came very readily to James. He admitted it was something that had remained very strongly in his memory, and which he stated that he occasionally mulled over even now.

The first situation that comes to mind was an incident at my previous school with a mother and her daughter. The child was the daughter of older parents who were quite protective of her. The parents came in to say that their daughter was being picked on and bullied. They claimed that she had been called names and spat on. I listened to them and said I would look into the situation and get back to them. When I had done so, I invited the parents into school. The mother and the daughter came. I explained that my investigations had discovered that the daughter was part of the problem and that she had caused it, partially, by name-calling. I was really trying to get to the truth. However, although the mother listened she didn't believe her daughter had done the things that I was suggesting. We had a good discussion about the events and I felt that we had agreed to differ, especially since the other child in the incident had apologised. Afterwards I felt it had been a very successful meeting, and that the mother had been supportive. However, within the week she sent in a letter of complaint suggesting that I was bullying her! I was very surprised not only because I thought the meeting had gone reasonably well but also because I was so used to dealing with this sort of situation as a headteacher. I felt that the parent did not like the view of the daughter that was being revealed. The whole incident has left an emotional scar. The official complaint made me wonder in all my next parent interviews 'What are people really thinking?' I spend a lot of time trying to pick up the pieces from incidents like this. The governors looked into the incident which in the end was the mother's word against mine. Finally, it was resolved by them all agreeing to differ and the child stayed at the school. I felt that the child never got the best out of her time in school. In a way I felt that I had failed and let them down. I learnt that being fair and open doesn't always work out. It has led to a certain reservation in what I now say to parents, and I am certainly more aware of body language.

There are various ways that an understanding of emotion and leadership could explain this incident. Some of his feelings could perhaps be explained because of his strong sense of fairness which was noted when we looked at his overall life story. He is clear about how much he values good relationships. Also, as an experienced head he felt he should have had the skills to work out this problem, but the emotions of all the participants were stronger than he had anticipated. He had to regulate his feelings at the time of the incident, but given that he stills mulls it over several years later, it would appear that it touched him particularly because his usual skills at reading others' emotions were not 'working'. Richardson might have argued that he had not seen that the mother was projecting her difficult feelings on to him.

George (2000) suggests that feelings play an important role in leadership because it is likely that a diversity of feelings influence leadership effectiveness. The tendency in telling stories about critical incidents was for the emphasis to be on the negative aspects. Negative emotions expressed in retelling incidents, George argues, can foster careful information processing (2000: 1031). This can be seen by all the recalled detail. These intense negative emotions may also act as signals to point the leader in the direction of the issue that requires immediate attention in that particular situation. In other words, this could be describing emotion-weighted decision-making.

One of the rare positive events (described to me by a head of a small primary school) was this:

> It was a school concert, and there were a group of parents standing waiting. I had been at the school about a year, and thought I knew enough to pick up vibes and knew you rarely get a committed opinion from anyone. A child came up to me in front of all the parents and said 'I am really glad that you came to this school', and the parents said so are we. It was an affirmation of what I was doing at the school, and what you believe in. It was just a group of parents, not the school association but an average group of parents. I felt it was initiated because the child had said it. I learnt that I needed affirmation, and that as a head you rarely got it. It was a really unsolicited recommendation of what you are doing.

This short incident uncovers several emotional aspects of leadership. What are the ones that you identify?

When is emotion apparent?

Many day-to-day events in schools would appear on the surface to be management tasks that make the organisation run more efficiently. As part of my research I spent several days in an infant school observing the very new headteacher, Ben. He had been a headteacher for less than a year, and when I first talked to him, only 50 days. Some examples of these sorts of tasks would be very familiar to you as a leader in primary or secondary schools:

- Ben 'touching base' with the school secretary throughout the day about matters ranging from supply teachers to proofreading letters for parents.
- Ben preparing the board for open day and taking photos for it at break time.
- Ben moving around school and grounds before the school day, and during the parents' evening.
- Ben answering letters and emails.

However, these tasks could also be viewed as only having meaning within the emotional context of the organisation. In other words, such apparently mundane tasks would only work well if the emotional context was conducive to it. Other tasks I observed could be viewed as more directly related to emotion:

- The seriously ill child: Ben realised the impact that a chronically ill child had on the staff and dealt with this both in terms of protocol (what they would do if the worst happened in school), and also the staff's feelings – arranging for them to have opportunities to discuss their feelings together or with trained colleagues.
- Close staff relationships, as shown by banter in staffroom, people asking Ben's view. In terms of headship as performance, he gave the appearance of calm to the staff and children, even although he was not always feeling that way, as he revealed when he talked to me.
- Good relationships on parents' evening: parents were free to express their views to Ben, and both parties listened to each other. It was mainly informal contact.

- Environment: the school was a calm, ordered and friendly place for the visitor. I suspect this is particularly important for the early years of schooling with both pupils and some parents being new to the context.

All these contextual aspects, imbued with emotion, are also very important to allow the core purpose of teaching and learning to happen for the children and the staff.

Observing Ben fulfilled two purposes for me. First, it confirmed the impression of Ben as an emotional being that I was building up in my mind from the interviews. He did consciously reflect on his emotions. By emotional being, I do not mean that he was exceptional as a headteacher in terms of being in tune with his own emotions and those of his staff. Rather, Ben was ready to acknowledge the emotion part of his role in a clear and consistent way. Second, it confirmed to me the importance of the interrelationship between the person and the social context. If I were to use a metaphor to analyse how Ben fitted into the school, it would seem to me that the idea of a 'comfy shoe' is very apt. He and the social context were working together. His leadership was enabled by the emotional context, and in return the emotional context enabled his leadership.

Stories and lives

It is very apparent from their lives and the stories that the heads tell that the affective side of leadership is very important to the context of the school. It does not matter whether they are male or female, experienced or inexperienced, in large or small schools. These stories reinforce the overall picture of the complexities of emotion, and the relationship between cognition and emotion, which is key to a more complete picture of leadership and emotion. I have given some specific examples but all of them made reference to their own belief systems, educational philosophy or core values drawn from their childhood experiences. The idea that headteachers can be emotional in pursuit of rational management objectives has not received much focus in the leadership literature, nor has the beneficial effects of negative emotion. As McLaughlin (2005) argues in his critical study of emotional intelligence as a concept, there is a risk of emotional development being disconnected from the wider aims of the school. Simplification of emotion to ignore the relationship between the cognitive and the affective is dangerous for the leader.

The importance of socialisation to the development of emotion (Matthews, Zeidner and Roberts, 2002), and leadership, is an important point which is also rarely argued in the leadership literature. The process of socialisation into teaching, and then into leadership roles, requires certain behaviours in public. As developing leaders, teaching staff learn certain ways of looking, sounding or even 'being'. The expectations of parents and children, perceived, or real, may reinforce this. These stories show emotion as a key part of the collective life of the school.

This process of emotion-shaping means that professionals and their client groups are complicit in defining the boundaries of what is, and is not, appropriate emotional display (Fineman, 2001: 227). Headteachers can unwittingly support the notion that ideal 'professional' behaviour is rational and carefully emotionally controlled when asked to talk about leadership behaviours. This may well be illusionary, as through the stories they tell outside the official process, the control aspect is emphasised, but not idealised by them. This process has been described as a recognition and understanding of the political environment created by emotions and the intricacies of managing it to make fundamental and deep-seated transformation (see James, 2000).

Conclusion

In terms of getting to the heart of leadership, the places we work are very relevant. They become part of a leader's overall emotional context, and in some difficult situations management of emotion may be a huge part of the leadership task. It's a large, complex, and compelling area for study for leaders, which you may like to read more about.

The concept of self-disclosure cuts across a number of subject disciplines. It relates closely to how people communicate with each other, both in personal relationships and also in organisational settings. Self-disclosure concerns how much about yourself as a person you are willing or able to reveal to others. It can be argued that the amount that you disclose influences your relationship with others, how people regard you, and the amount of self-knowledge that you yourself possess (Derlerga and Berg, 1987). Trust and relationships can be built up through such reciprocity. Generally, there is only a small relationship between how good we believe we are at understanding others and how much we really know about them. However, the whole area of self-disclosure and also social identity are apposite areas for leaders in education to become more knowledgeable about. I will return to the subject of self-disclosure when discussing sustainability in Chapter Eight.

Social identity and 'being a headteacher' are explored further in the next chapter. In terms of the life narrative of leaders, much of teaching is in groups, teams and informal work-task groups. Our social identity is built in groups. Teachers are involved in formal and informal groups within a school. They maintain the status of their group by valuing it above others, often because the membership has an emotional value. The interesting thing to note in terms of our emotional well-being is that group membership is important to most people. So group membership is as important for leaders as it is for the staff in a school, but may be expressed in different and often subtle ways. Group membership for leaders is also more difficult in a high stakes, accountability culture. As the role of leader in education is taken on, so membership of many of these groups can become problematic. Identity theory would suggest that headteachers have to value the importance of continuity with their past as they progress into their new role (Erikson, 1980).

Think points

1 Note down one positive and one negative critical incident that you have experienced as an educational leader. Describe the context, your reaction and that of others, and what happened afterwards. What did you learn from these about yourself and the organisation? Is it the same incident you noted in Chapter One?
2 Which have been the most significant groups you have belonged to in your career? What, if any, was the emotional component?
3 Think of the first headteacher you ever worked for. How did s/he display emotion? What was the effect of this in terms of the emotional context of the school?
4 Do you agree that self-disclosure is important for leaders to understand? Can you think of an example that justifies your answer?

Further reading

Delerga, V. and Berg, J. (eds) (1987) *Self-Disclosure: Theory, Research and Therapy*. New York: Springer.
If you are interested in aspects of self-disclosure, you may want to read about it in more depth.

Fineman, S. (ed.) (2000) *Emotion in Organizations*. London: Sage.

Fineman S. (ed.) (2008) *The Emotional Organization*. Oxford: Blackwell.
For more detailed reading about emotion in organisations and how society influences the way we view emotion (emotionology), these two books are very useful.

Russell, M. (2003) 'Leadership and followership as a relational process', *Educational Management and Administration*, 31 (2): 145–57.
This article helps extend the focus of your thinking to followership in particular.

Sugrue, C. (2005) 'Putting "real life" into school leadership; connecting leadership, identities and life history', in C. Sugrue (ed.) *Passionate Principalship*. London: RoutledgeFalmer.
I have selected just this chapter but the whole book is dedicated to looking at how leadership and life connect.

Chapter 7

Being a headteacher

> ## Introduction
>
> This chapter looks at what 'being a headteacher' means in the context of today's schools. It takes the view that the social power of emotion shapes the work of headteachers and how this social power is shaped and moulded by the work that schools do. At the heart of it all are relationships. At the same time, I will argue that being a headteacher also has a personal component that is shaped by the leadership narrative and is part of one's individual identity as a teacher and leader in schools.

The best we have to offer

Speaking about effective primary heads, Whitaker (1997) suggests that such headteachers help to create the conditions in which people will want to work to the optimum levels of their energy, interest and commitment. This is similar to the concept that the NCSL used in the Leadership Programme for Serving Heads (LPSH), which they call discretionary effort, where people are willing to 'go the extra mile' for others in the team or group within which they work. Whitaker sees leadership as something which:

> will create the conditions in which *the best we have to offer* [my emphasis] can effectively be harnessed in the face of difficulties and obstacles. (1997: 127)

Educational leadership training has usefully developed emotional intelligence (EI) and the idea of emotional competences, and this has proved helpful to many people in leadership roles in schools. At the same time, writers have argued that this new interest in emotion has moved leaders from the 'myth of rationality' to the 'myth of emotion' (Hatcher, 2008). As Hatcher succinctly puts it:

> the new 'emotion' valued in organisations is not so much about care and connection as it is about an objective determination about how to 'perform' appropriate emotion and to express it in such a way as to deliver results: the competence of emotion. (2008: 164)

My contention is that headteachers that do the job well emphasise 'care and connection' with their educational values and are able to nurture that in others. Care and connection can lead to high performance but may not be sustainable in the longer term. The heads in my study were able to 'perform' but never at the detriment of their own educational values because they supported, and were supported by, their staff. This relationship is important to being a headteacher because when this is altered in some way by life events, even the most capable headteachers can lose their ability to work well. This two-way nature of the emotional context of leadership meant that these particular heads were able to maintain their focus on teaching and learning. Their work was sustainable because it did not ask them to move beyond the boundaries of emotional comfort, and allowable expression of feelings. Also, none of them were faced by some of the more difficult or unsolvable emotional problems that can influence sustainability. This aspect will be covered in Chapter Eight.

Leadership development

I have argued that a social view of emotion is very important for leaders to understand, because belonging to groups is so much a part of education. Understanding the emotional context is vital for anyone in a leadership position. For an even more complete picture of themselves as 'being a headteacher', I believe that knowledge of the different perspectives that there are in emotion research would enhance the skills that heads have when faced with difficulties and obstacles. Some of these issues could be addressed in leadership development.

It has been suggested (Earley and Weindling, 2004: 174) that examples of good practice in leadership development from around the world include learning theories, mentoring and coaching, reflection, problem-based learning and case studies, action learning, storytelling and drama, journals, e-learning and learning communities. Some of these are more embedded in the leadership development of heads than others. For example, mentoring and coaching, e-learning and learning communities are currently prevalent in both courses from private providers and the NCSL (Bush and Glover, 2004). The difficulty with matters to do with emotion is that which I have reiterated throughout this book; emotion and leadership can be viewed as difficult territory, where the knowledge base in educational leadership is only now developing fully. Some of the methods outlined above, such as storytelling and drama, reflection and journals, could be seen to have particular relevance to emotion and educational leadership. They have been used in research successfully (Ginsberg and Davies, 2002), and could certainly be used to explore emotional issues in leadership. For example, the Lupton (1998) categorisation is a useful aid to thinking, and was the basis of the three emotional textures that I outlined: emotional regulation in leadership; emotion-weighted decision-making; and emotional context. Together they add to a head's emotional coherence as a leader. It means that educational leaders can realise that although there may be a cognitive rationale for actions, there is an underlying and probably stronger affective rationale, even though emotion may not be apparent on the surface.

In a fundamental sense, headteachers are moved to action by their feelings (Gabriel, 1999). Dillard (1995) also argues that leaders not only use their experiences to lead, but they lead from themselves as people, their past experiences and their personalities and life experiences. For some head-teachers, due to any or all of these factors, any display of emotion, either in themselves or others, may be perceived as inappropriate for educational leaders.

Moeller argues that over the last 10 years there has been a move to view teaching as an emotional practice, which has been partially reflected in the leadership literature, par-ticularly in an acknowledgement that one cannot separate feeling from perception and judgement (2005: 90). It has also been partially reflected in training.

The emotional coherence of leadership could be a fruitful focus for headteacher development and training in several areas. For example, educational leadership research (Duke, 1998; Goddard, 1998; Gronn and Ribbins, 1996; Southworth, 2004) consistently notes the importance of context. More understanding of emotional coherence could draw on pres-ent work about context, bringing together the personal and the socially constructed perspectives. Also, given the impor-tance of emotional regulation, developing heads' conceptual knowledge of emotional labour could help them with emo-tionally coherent leadership. Parts of headteacher training, such as coaching and mentoring, look at this implicitly. It could be developed more proactively conceptually so that headteachers have knowledge of both emotional labour and emotional wounding. They could also look at what these ideas mean both for coherence and for long-term sustainability. This work could be carried out through group work with cohorts of heads at different times in their career, allowing them access to some of the deeper emotional epiphanies and emotional wounds that they may have experienced. Helpful, positive ways of handling key critical incidents with an emotional component could also be shared. The personal leadership narrative could also be utilised to discuss aspects of the affective in the context of the current school in which they work. This has implications for the training of effective facilitators, as they require particular skills if such work is not to be seen as either too difficult or not worth spending time on because it only covers the surface of emotion and leadership. The idea of an emotional transaction is, I think, a useful one for headteachers to bear in mind when faced with difficult management situations, but is also an area where cognitive and emotional aspects of leadership could be proactively examined.

Becoming more emotionally coherent

In creating emotional coherence, coaching will have a role to play, although training may need to take into account more counselling-focused skills. Howe (1993: 140) suggests that leaders draw on three key ingredients in emotional transactions:

1 Acceptance (a secure emotional base for the relationship)
2 Understanding (an appreciation of the other person's felt experience)

3 Dialogue (the communication of understanding and meaning).

When this is touched upon in headteacher development and training it can be very powerful in terms of self-reflection for the headteacher. As with emotional intelligence, there is the danger that the power of self-knowledge may either be reduced to competency assessment, or that the trainers are unable or insufficiently trained to move the reflection on beyond self-absorption.

Knowing and expressing how their emotional coherence as a headteacher is sustained could also provide a powerful tool for personal reflection. As Hargreaves suggests:

> Teachers don't just have jobs. They have professional and personal lives as well. Although it seems trite to say this, many failed efforts in in-service training, teacher development and educational change more widely are precisely attributable to this neglect of the teacher as a person. (Hargreaves, 1994: viii)

The headteacher as an emotional being is neglected in a target-driven accountability culture in education. The personal and professional lives of headteachers are inextricably entwined, yet they sit within an educational culture in many countries that takes no account of this. The quote above could apply just as much to a headteacher as to a teacher.

Educational leaders are often aware of the pivotal, and I would argue, emotional, role that they can play in an organisation. Earley and Weindling conclude that:

> Distributed and shared leadership, whilst welcome, still rely heavily on leadership, alongside effective management, being successfully demonstrated at the *apex* of the organisation. (2004: 183)

The headteachers in my study were very much at the apex of their schools, whilst advocating shared leadership with their staff. In terms of training and development, the message that came through from the interviews was of the importance of the personal in headship. This accords with Richardson's idea of the headteacher being the person in the school who spans many boundaries. He or she is nominally at the apex, but also has to work in different ways with many stakeholders. The key difference since Richardson's work is that headteachers are held to account for hard results in a way that she did not conceive, even if the emotional context of the school conspires against this being a realistic possibility for any headteacher.

Returning to my research into schools in challenging circumstances, being a headteacher was very much affected by the emotional concerns of parents, staff and students. In many ways, their humanity, and explicit acknowledgement of the personal, emotional aspects of headship in such a context helped staff to move forward in their own emotional journeys.

Personal reflection on 'being a headteacher'

I am not arguing that the headteachers I interviewed were not organisation focused, for they were. It is to note that many of them, especially in the primary sector, outlined ways in which they yearned to be able to share more of the emotional side of leadership with others, without being judged. The high accountability framework within which headship is situated means that there are very few 'safe' emotional spaces for heads. James pinpointed this when he remarked that he used to be able to talk to his link advisor about anything that was bothering him when he first became a head 15 or so years ago, but now almost the first words of his advisor are: 'How are you getting on with raising the Key Stage 2 SATS results?' This is an oversimplification, but it ties in with creating space in training and development for heads, where they can discuss and reflect on the personal and emotional. I will look at this in more detail below.

Whitaker puts it well when he says that we need to challenge the principle that people and how they are treated is one of the least significant factors for consideration in schools (1997: 144). From this study, I would say that this applies particularly to primary heads (mainly women), and the figures on the low number of applicants for primary headships, and people wanting to progress to headship, would seem to bear this out (GTCE, 2006; Howson, 2005). To paraphrase Whitaker (ibid.), what is so abusive about schools is the appalling waste of human talent they preside over. This is a strong statement, but researching into emotional and educational leadership has suggested to me that recruitment difficulties etc. are much easier to discuss 'rationally' than relating so many of these problems to the more problematic relationship of emotion and educational leadership. It is a difficult discussion to have. For example, as I write this book, I know of three headteachers, who have been successful in the school system for many years, having to leave headship due to various factors which have altered their context – a critical Ofsted report; chronic illness caused by stress; changes in the school demographics leading to more challenges. All of these contextual changes have led to three people moving from being admired headteachers, lauded by their local authorities, Ofsted, and government ministers, to the twenty-first century equivalent of a social leper. Their careers have ended without any regard for their person, and yet we seem to not understand the unwillingness of younger teachers to take on the headship role.

As a school governor, I have worked with both primary and secondary heads dealing with issues such as murder, suicide, affairs among the staff, stealing from the school (staff), excluding five-year-olds permanently, child abuse, and chronic or extreme illness among pupils, parents or staff, to name but a few. Sometimes these events and their emotional aftermath took up a huge degree of management time. Some heads were emotionally well-equipped to deal with these incidents, and were supported in the school or the local authority. Others would have welcomed an acknowledgement that the cumulative effects of such emotional containment were that they felt even more physically exhausted. While dealing with some of these events, one headteacher commented that it would make no difference to Ofsted how he handled such incidents, as they only wanted to know about the A–Cs at GCSE, and would certainly not take into account such things. At its extreme it can lead to headteachers valuing external accountability above people, even though they knew it was not 'right' to do so. An example of a head asking a teaching assistant to come in anyway for Ofsted (although her mother had died that morning) illustrates this. This is not to argue that the personal is not valued, as equally there are examples where headteachers, and indeed Ofsted inspectors have valued the personal, but it is more and more difficult for them to do so. Any developments for headteachers would need to be finely crafted to tackle such a difficult area, within a safe environment.

Becoming a headteacher

I want to, briefly, suggest some ways in which leadership development could be enriched. These could include:

- Introducing more in-depth knowledge of research into emotion, not just emotional intelligence. Emotional intelligence, whilst a useful acknowledgement of skills in this area, is often reduced to a competency approach. Also, it is a relatively easy and safe way to approach a difficult area, and makes a useful starting point. Deeper knowledge of some of the other perspectives on emotion would enrich headteachers as they tackle ever more complex leadership situations within a framework where they are more and more accountable.

- Acknowledgement of the difficulties of emotion and leadership, alongside proactive solutions. Understanding the nuances of emotion and leadership could encourage educational leaders to acknowledge some of the areas that have been discussed in this book and how they apply to their own leadership. Getting to the heart of leadership would mean allowing themselves to use their cognitive, rational capacity to ask 'What is going on emotionally in this situation?'

- Reflections on the personal in pre, post and longer-term headship. I have argued that both life history and its development into the personal leadership narrative is a useful tool for educational leaders. It allows them to examine how they are shaping their own story of leadership, and the part that emotion plays in their efficacy as a leader.

- Emotional management and its relationship to emotional context and overall coherence. This is an area in which there could be a wealth of development, especially at various stages of a leadership journey. Some headteachers will be temperamentally more able to 'act the head' and not show emotion. Others will find that they are not actually aware of how they manage their emotions, or do it in ways that are not good for their long-term mental or physical health. Having a coherent understanding of what 'being a headteacher' means emotionally is a key element for anyone wishing to get to the heart of leadership in schools.

Development of these areas would be demanding. This challenge is one that is worthwhile, and could be developed alongside the current interests in positive psychology and happiness (Gladwell, 2005; Layard, 2005; Seligman, Park and Peterson, 2005) that are developing in the wider research and policy arena. For example, Layard (2005: 113) suggests that if we want to measure the quality of people's lives, such measurement must be based on the way people feel. It is not possible for those in leadership positions to be happy all the time, but if the headteacher is the emotional pivot of the school, then their happiness should be a major consideration.

An illustration of 'being a head' – Ben, a new head

An illustration of the quality of people's lives can be seen if I re-introduce Ben, the headteacher with whom I spent several days in school. Although I already 'knew' Ben, that is I had come across him on a training course I led, I learnt a great deal about him that I did not know – his childhood in particular was a surprise to me, as was the depth of feeling with which he told his story. This was the longest interview that I conducted in the study, and it highlighted for me that the appearance of competence at leadership in a work setting is underpinned by emotional labour. This labour is apparently far greater for some people than others, and relates to both the past and the present context of their lives, within an educational climate that does not often allow the personal to become visible. Visibility can open up a headteacher to criticism, of 'being emotional' and also not being able to cope. Ironically, this labour means that by the time that the headteacher has admitted their inability to keep up the labour under pressure, it may be too late for their physical and mental well-being (Ashforth and Tomiuk, 2000; Carlyle and Woods, 2002; West-Burnham and Ireson, 2006).

James and Eleanor had talked about the differences in support for them between when they started as heads and the present day. Eleanor mentioned that if she had a magic wand and could be given anything she needed to help her as a head-teacher, she would ask for a confidential support person to whom she could talk without fear of judgement or comeback of any kind. This insight was developed further with Ben, who found it useful, he said, to have me to reflect on things with, without any danger of being thought in some way inadequate. Here you have a duality of leadership and emotion in educa-tion. Emotional labour is needed at greater and greater levels in order to present the accepted rational front to stakehold-ers, which means that the headteacher does not feel able to stop the labour, and at the same time, there are very few available people professionally with whom he/she could share the difficulties of the job. Ben was also a rare male head-teacher in a school for the under-sevens. His leadership nar-rative goes some way towards explaining this.

Ben was someone who I had been introduced to on a training course for deputies at his previous school. Temperamentally, he was the most reserved of the case study heads, and of course the least experienced (90 days as a head). Hearing that he had just taken up his headship made me interested to include him as one of the case study head-teachers, because the very early years were unrepresented in the study. As you read it, try to examine your own emo-tional reactions to the story he tells.

Childhood and schooling

Ben is originally from Southern England. His early memories of school are to do with a teacher with white hair, and later a teacher with a bandage on her ankle. He also remembers lots of wood and the desks. This was his first school, and he transferred at seven to a brand new primary, which was being built in his area. He remembers it as 'horrible', and can't recall how long he was there, perhaps a year. He had a male teacher who made him stand on a table, and asked the class to point when he had problems with his bladder. He remembers thinking that this should not be happening to a child and it is something he tries to remember as a teacher. One of the items that stands out in memory from that particular incident was that teacher's hair in particular, possibly because he was on a table at the time. When he thinks about the school, he knows that he made friends there, and also recalls making a robot with cereal packets. He didn't tell his parents how unhappy he was, but once they did realise, they removed him. He can't remember the details of this. His older sister was working at a small prep school locally, and he went there for an interview and went in to the second form there in January for a term. He stayed there until he was 13, even though his sister left after he started there. Ben recalls that he felt much happier there generally and was involved in many aspects of the school. At the same time there was more academic pressure – to try to get a scholarship at 13 and go to boarding school. This pressure did not come from home, he thought that it came from the school. He got through the Common Entrance Exam and went to a local direct grant school in a large town. His primary had been very small and there he was always first or second at everything. In contrast, his secondary school was large, and Ben found that some of the subject content was very different (maths, science). It was then he began to 'switch off' and he remembers his reports mentioning how little effort he put in. He got five O levels, but managed somehow to miss his French exam which displeased the head, and he had to do the retake in November. For A levels he studied French, English and history and he really enjoyed them although he struggled with French. He wanted to go to university to do an English language degree and thought he would manage a B and a D in his other subjects, but he didn't. He had no real career plan at this stage. The headteacher suggested that polytechnics were an option, but Ben says that at the time he felt they were not proper universities. So, he knew then that he would have to get a job.

Ben conjures up a keen sense of people and place in his

memories of early childhood: people's hair, bandages, wood, desks. Negative emotions are to the forefront. His unhappy time has great detail in it, redolent of shame and failure, encapsulated in his memory of a significant personal incident, which has resulted in a strong sense of fairness for children in his current role. Educational values, possibly transferred from his parents and privileged schooling, feature strongly in his story, both in terms of how his experiences influenced him as a teacher, and also him thinking that polytechnics were not quite the places for him to be.

The next step

Ben had no idea what he should do with his life post-school, and his parents did not push him in any particular direction. He got a job at his father's firm working as a trainee buyer, and after six months of training moved to two different towns in the county. He would go back to his hometown at weekends and meet up with his friends who were all at university – he went to stay with friends who were at Oxford, for example. He still had no desire to do anything else, and admits that he was lazy at this period! Then, his father had to move to another town as the hometown branch was closed, and his home base was disrupted, as there was not really much space for him in the new house. He was by now getting fed up with his job (they had had a change of manager which he felt influenced him), and he got offered another job that was based in his hometown. He started work there as a trainee transport manager but it soon became obvious to him that he did not have the experience to deal with the mostly older drivers. He gave up work, and went back to his parents, sharing a small room, and did nothing at all for several months. He had no idea what to do, and no thought as to what he could be good at. He wondered, as his parents had always been involved in fostering, whether he should consider social work as an option. Then he looked at his options as a mature student at university and the idea of a sociology degree appealed. He had a friend at university in the north of England, and went and looked around. So he eventually went to university in his twenties. He had a great time, but in retrospect he can see that he was still coasting. The return to academic work was difficult and he took a while to settle in, but he enjoyed most of the lectures, and got into football. He even borrowed friends' stuff to get him through exams. A crucial moment for him was when he was studying the sociology of education, he got a placement at a local state nursery that he really enjoyed. He feels he was used to younger children through his family and fostering. Then he got really interested in his dissertation when it was suggested to him that he could do it about football hooliganism. He got a good grade for this. He decided that as he enjoyed working with children, he would apply to do a 3–8 PGCE at a major red brick university. He hated his first day in school but the second placement, in a nursery, was much better. He met his wife on the course. His last placement was also a struggle as the teacher found it hard to leave him alone with the class; he had to be moderated before he passed.

Unlike the other heads in this study, Ben worked before going to university because of his poor A level results, and a sense that he had no idea what to do with his life. When he did get to university it appears to have been a very significant time in his development; he talked about his time there in much greater detail than all the others, probably as his schooling and early career were less successful than the others'. In fact, all through his education, he draws a picture of someone whose confidence not only went up and down, with what he regarded as significant failures, but of someone who had strong family support, even when he felt he had let them down. This is reinforced in the next part of his narrative, where he has a 'rough' year, a head he 'didn't rate', and felt 'close to chucking it in'.

Ben applied for several education 'pools', and in the end both he and his wife got a job at the same school. Unfortunately, the head had mental illness problems, and had significant periods of absence. The deputy was very bitter about the head, and this made for an unpleasant atmosphere, mitigated only a little by the deputy's dry sense of humour. It was a difficult probationary year, with very little support, in what Ben termed an 'unstable atmosphere'. In the end, he discussed his difficulties with the chair of governors, and also the local education authority. Nothing seemed to change, so he decided to resign and move on. It was very turbulent at the school, as three other staff had already gone. He then got a job in Essex for a year, at a school which was going through a change of head. He then got an A allowance at another primary school for two and a half years. The head there was 'a bit of a Will Scarlett!' (showman), it was a big school but well organised and friendly. This headteacher then left, and the new head appointed Ben 'didn't rate'. He was from a 'Christian/scouting' background and Ben felt that he didn't have the staff's interests at heart. By then he and his wife wanted to relocate, and chose where they wanted to go, and wrote to all the schools in that town. His wife got a job at a middle school, and he in the feeder first. Then the schools combined and he found the head not supportive, and 'insecure', he felt that 'you never knew where you were with her.' Also, she did not tackle ineffective teachers. He was now in charge of maths, but had a very difficult class at the same time. He felt close to chucking it all in at this point. In the end, he decided to apply for deputy headships. He had five interviews, which he didn't get, and then was approached to be acting deputy at a Catholic school. Although he is not religious they were looking for someone who could teach Year 2. He found the atmosphere at this school completely different and loved it there. He felt the staff and the head were dedicated to their jobs, and did them with humour. The head was also willing to stand up for what she believed and challenge people. He would love to have stayed, and the governors explored the possibility, but as he was not a Catholic, it was not possible. He was offered the opportunity to stay for another year if he had wanted it. He began to look around for other deputy headships. He saw a new school post advertised, and he liked the headteacher, and he got it. And, of course, he is now the head.

Headship

Ben was in his first year of headship when he was inter-viewed (and the start of his second when he was observed). Again, his teaching career path has a strong sense of ups and downs. Thematically, it can be seen that the *relationships* in all the schools appear to be crucial in getting the best out of him, and healing past difficulties. This may be to do with his own emotions and sense of *fairness* and *self and self-esteem*. Some of this can also be seen in the other life history sto-ries, for example, James and his secondary school pathway, see pp. 53–4), and would suggest that self-esteem is an important part of the emotional context that makes up headship.

Observing Ben also reaffirmed the idea of the importance of emotional context. The emotional context of the school – the relationships within, both public and private – elides and interfaces with the inner emotional context of the head-teacher. Waldron, when discussing relational and emotional experiences at work, notes that 'all organisational emotion is relational' (2000: 65). This is true of emotional labour and support for heads as discussed above. As Waldron suggests the interdependent nature of work roles in some organisa-tions (such as schools) creates the need for collective emo-tional performance. The idea of collective emotional performance reflects the emotional side of teaching. Waldron suggests that certain kinds of emotion are experi-enced because people have to work so closely together (2000: 66). As he puts it:

> Private and public dimensions of work are in constant tension … at work, relationship violations can be humili-atingly public … [this] can have the effect of intensifying emotional reactions' (2000: 67).

Mary and the difficult teacher would be a good example of this (p. 27). Waldron puts it succinctly when he notes that emotion has the power to define obligation to others in the workplace, and that one of its functions may be to define the boundaries between formal and informal rights (ibid.: 71). So, in the school, Ben would have the right as headteacher to point out errors, as he did, gently but firmly when one teacher was not able to manage the timings at parents' evening effectively. Her emotional reaction to this was crucial in how others that were in the area at the time (the whole centre of the school is a large shared workspace), interpreted Ben's skills as a leader, and whether this was appropriate. Because of shared obligations on parents' evening timings, and the emotional context of the school, this public incident was accepted by the teacher as being a learning experience. Afterwards the whole experience was laughed off in the company of other teachers, which of course may be a social defence in itself.

Although Ben was a new headteacher, he was not new to the school, and the comfort levels of all the people I saw him deal with were high. As Fineman notes, 'emotions are inter-subjective, a product of the way systems of meaning are created and negotiated between people' (2000: 2). The emotional context of Pennington was such (Ben and staff started together in this brand-new school) that Ben was able to behave as naturally or authentically as anyone can in a professional context. This enabled him to utilise emotion as a tool to maintain good workplace relationships, as long as it was seen to be genuine by the other staff. A good example of this was his concern for the very sick child, and the systems he was putting in place to support the staff, and help them to move forward in the event of the child dying at school. Genuine emotions can release emotional tension, and also signal to staff, parents and students the presence of relational trust and acceptance of each other's individuality (Waldron, 2000: 74–5).

Telling your story

Narrative and the power of story have featured strongly in this book, both in terms of the tales people tell about themselves and others (collective stories), and also in my overall writing approach, which in many senses tells a story about emotion and leadership. How do we emotionally construct ourselves? This question is more than this particular book can answer. Ben, when discussing past failures and how these were resolved, found the act of *telling* the story helpful in its own right. You might like to explore this idea in further reading about the psychology of emotion.

Ben's story reminded me strongly of the view expressed earlier by Briner that emotion occurs in the context of our personal history, past, present and anticipated future. Encouraging the headteachers to tell me stories about their lives, unconsciously led them to tell me what I have termed their own 'personal leadership narrative'. The power of the personal leadership narrative, or the story that leaders tell about themselves and how it influences their own leadership of others, is underlined by Ben's story.

Ben's personal leadership narrative is not just the facts of his personal history. His personal story influences the leadership narrative in subtle emotional ways. His unhappy childhood, low self-esteem as a teenager and parental values have been utilised by him to create a different situation for the children in his care, especially when he was first teaching. His leadership narrative indicates a striving for authenticity as a leader. Notions of authenticity are contested in the psychological literature. The definition that is most relevant is given by Ashforth and Tomiuk who define authenticity as the extent to which a person behaves according to what they consider to be their true and genuine self (2000: 184). Although such definitions are bound by deeper questions about what is the self, and whether authenticity is contextual in itself, this definition struck me as particularly relevant to headteachers. Helen Gunter (1999) notes that the headteacher's professional identity may be an intrinsic part of a person's life more generally. The idea of a personal leadership narrative takes this further. It enables the head-teacher to believe in the authenticity of their leadership by valuing themselves in the context of the narrative that they have woven. A personal leadership narrative can enhance or decrease their subjective emotional well-being.

Ben's personal leadership narrative leads him to believe in the power of relationships to move people forward and that it is through supportive relationships that he has become a stronger person, teacher, father and headteacher. His leadership narrative is authentic to him but shows the way that the concept of the self can fluctuate over time. When he was first interviewed, he was only just beginning to be a headteacher. By the time of the observation, his surface acting (Hochschild, 1983) of the role of headteacher had developed into a deeper identity of headteacher, and was, as such, authentic to him.

Conclusion

The concept of a personal leadership narrative emphasises that the individual must attend to how they feel about themselves as leaders. This affective part of their leadership influences how they engage with the feelings of others within the social context of the school. The narrative encompasses many facets of their past, and it aids reflection on you as a person. After in-depth interviewing of head-teachers, Pascal and Ribbins noted:

> It doesn't matter how many courses you've been on, and how much you know intellectually about the process of being a head if you don't develop an appreciation of your-self as a person … you will never make a good head. (1998: 22)

Narratives are a powerful tool to help headteachers make

some of their implicit personal values explicit, both to themselves and others.

Personal histories remain relatively under-explored in headship, although there are some good examples, such as the work of Pascal and Ribbins, 1998. I would argue that there is a place for more exploration. The whole area of identity is a rich one for the educational leader to explore, and my approach is influenced by the particular stance I take towards identity. I consider that a person's emotional identity influences their personal educational leadership narrative, because personal and social identities are very closely related. Sarbin (1989) calls this 'storied lives', and it is this idea that I feel is very useful in exploring leadership and contextual fit. It is precisely the idea that identity is not static that makes this interchange between the educational leader and the context so interesting to explore. Fineman notes that identity 'is a process of holding and resolving different social–emotional narratives about who we are, who we were, and who we wish to be' (2008: 5). 'Being a headteacher' is more than just a role, although the understanding of that role is crucial. This chapter suggests that understanding how emotion relates to the personal and the social identity is a valuable piece of knowledge for a headteacher. How this identity is shaped and changed by the context of work and the telling of the story is vital to being a leader in schools.

Think point

There is only one think point for this chapter. Using the leadership narratives of the headteachers in this book as a guide, what does 'being a headteacher' mean to you? What are the key emotional events that have helped form you as a person and as an educational leader?

Further reading

Day, C., Stobart, G., Sammons, P., Kington, A. and Gu, Q. (2006) *Variations in Teachers' Work, Lives and Effectiveness. Research Report 743*. Nottingham: Department for Education and Skills.
This interesting study looks at teachers' work, and links, for me, to the idea of a leadership narrative.

Gabriel, Y. (2000) *Storytelling in Organizations: Facts, Fiction, and Fantasies*. Oxford: Oxford University Press.
This book gives a different viewpoint on the role of story-telling in organisations that is very relevant to schools.

Chapter 8

Looking forward

Introduction

This chapter looks forward to how developments in education today may alter the emotional context for educational leaders. It asks whether headteachers will still have a pivotal emotional role. In considering the future, I will also reiterate the importance of the personal in the leadership narrative and its connection with sustainability in headship.

There is no doubt that the policy context for headteachers in all parts of the United Kingdom has altered substantially over the last 20 years. Research in leadership has apparently moved away from the person of the headteacher to concepts that seek to use the talents of all in the school. Concepts such as distributed leadership; teacher leadership and system leadership have all had a role to play in focusing attention away from headteachers. Partly this is because such concepts are an effective way to focus on how to manage groups of people, and partly it is due to the impossibility of one person shouldering the burden of leadership over a sustained period. At the same time, schools have had to embrace other policy issues such as the ECM (Every Child Matters) agenda, and the advent of early years centres. The government continues to increase the accountability of schools via their headteachers. This can limit the style and extent of shared leadership within schools

– itself a source of anxiety and ambiguity for staff and school leaders.

Over the same period, the leadership literature, as concerned with education, has grown and developed, often seen to be focusing on groups, teams, and how teachers can be leaders. This literature has been influenced by the school effectiveness and school improvement research, and has influenced many aspects of practice in both secondary and primary schools. It is also easy to view the language of management as innately rational if, for example, targets and accountability are studied on their own. Many countries have brought in headteacher preparation programmes, and programmes for advanced leaders. Yet in both England and Scotland, the number of applicants for primary headship, for example, has fallen. Why should this be? Research that a colleague and I have carried out (Cowie and Crawford, 2007) suggests that it is not because headteachers perceive their preparation as inadequate, although there may be room for improvement. Perhaps, part of the reason, as suggested in the last chapter, is that the headteachers' social identity has not been considered enough. There are many efforts to change this situation as I write, and it may well be that finding the leaders of the future at a young age, and nurturing them is part of the way forward. Knowledge of the affective side of both yourself and the organisation is also paramount.

Organisational culture

Throughout the book, I have argued that the educational leadership literature points at a growing awareness of the affective dimension of leadership within organisations and in schools in particular. Educational leadership is fundamentally about people, and people necessarily work in an emotional context, intrapersonally and interpersonally. In an article that argues for a refocus on the organisation in the study of educational leadership, Glatter suggests that we look more closely at what the main tasks of a school are:

> We should consciously seek to contribute to ... the broader field of organization and management studies, in which ... schools and universities can be viewed – along for example with churches, counselling agencies, hospitals and prisons – as *human service organizations* whose core task is transforming humans. (2006: 82)

Looking forward, and in considering different or dispersed forms of leadership in the future, I think this concentration on organisations is helpful. The focus on the organisation itself and not on leadership, per se, is something that researchers in organisations have been exploring for some time. As Fineman puts it clearly:

> The emotional field is one the organizational researcher can explore with some joy. It contains an abundance of conceptual riches, which, with wise use, can transform our rather grey and tidy picture of people in organizations to one which ranges in emotional colour, passion and individual purpose. (1995: 223)

Emotion and leadership are in danger currently of becoming 'grey and tidy' by an overemphasis on competence and emotion, and one way to bring back 'colour' and 'purpose' is to look at how individuals and the organisation relate to each other emotionally.

There are many differences of view about how far organisational culture exists and what it comprises (Bennett, 1995; Morgan, 1998). It is an area you might wish to study further in the follow up readings. Cultures can be viewed as socially constructed realities (Berger and Luckmann, 1991), where members of an organisation may share basic assumptions and beliefs. These operate unconsciously. Levenson's definition of culture is that it 'not only creates the social world, it guides people in the affective reactions needed to function in that world' (1999: 513). He defines culture as a community of shared meanings. It is as if these shared meanings are bound by the affective relationships within the group. This is very similar to the way Elizabeth Richardson describes sentient groups. Levenson suggests, as Richardson does, that emotion can help individuals to define group boundaries. Social anxiety, for example, can motivate people to avoid behaviours that would have them evicted from the group. This might be at the cost of more effective group or task performance. He views collective emotional behaviour as a way of solidifying group bonds and negotiating group-related problems (1999: 512). It is recognising this that is particularly helpful to educational leaders. The primary function of emotion in this case is to serve as a signal that helps us clarify our views. It has been noted already that institutional feelings will alter behaviour, because of the importance of the emotional context of the school. Put another way:

> Emotional patterns and reasons behind our dealings with each other in organisations help us to picture the emotional spaces between and within people. ((Beatty, 2002: 73)

The idea of 'between and within' reflects the idea of 'being a headteacher' and taking into account the headteacher's personal feelings as well as shown emotion in dealing with various groups in school. It seems then that emotion can influence culture and vice versa. The definition of what culture is and how cultures change depends on how one perceives and enacts culture (Meyerson and Martin, 1997). At the extreme of this argument, it could be suggested that almost all structures within schools can only be interpreted through the emotions, beliefs, values and behaviours of the people involved (Leithwood, Jantzi and Steinbach, 1999: 71–2) in creating and enacting them. If the culture of an organisation is created and sustained at least partly by the emotions of the participants, it is important that those in leadership roles seek to understand their own and others' emotions. As the nature of these educational organisations changes with the advent of new policies, so leaders will experience a variety of conflicting feelings that will affect their emotional response to the organisations in which they work.

What lies ahead emotionally?

Hargreaves talks of teaching as having a set of specific emotional 'expectations, contours, and effects' (2000: 2). He sets out a conceptual framework for what he calls emotional *geographies* of teaching. Teachers and leaders are socialised within these expectations, and as the nature of the work changes, does the basic emotional geography change? I want to look briefly at two examples of areas of leadership where the work of leaders is changing, or it is suggested that it should change.

One of these areas is system leadership. Hopkins argues that there is 'a necessity for outstanding leadership as a system as a whole grapples with the challenge of adaptive change' (2007: 152). He identifies four drivers of system reform – personalised learning, professionalised teaching, intelligent accountability and networking and innovation, and argues that it is system leadership that will maximise the impact of these. System leaders, Hopkins says, are those leaders who 'care about and work for the success of other schools as well as their own' (ibid.: 153). Care is, of course, an affective description. Hopkins talks of empowering communities and moral purpose. There is not space to give full justice to his arguments here. You may wish to read more, and the details are given in the further reading. Hopkins is arguing for a different way of looking at leadership in order to respond both to challenges in society, and also to the needs of the future. Given that one of the descriptors used above is to empower communities, there must be considerable scope to look at how this will affect the emotional context of school leadership. Such empowerment brings increasing demands in terms of leadership and emotion. Looking at the idea of system leadership through some of the various perspectives outlined in previous chapters could lead to some productive research and discussion on such aspects as the boundaries of the organisation and the social relationships of larger groups. Emotionally, does system leadership take more or less account of the personal heart of leadership? Such issues will become increasingly relevant if system leadership is to have the impact that Hopkins argues for.

Another policy, which is making a considerable difference in terms of practice, is the Every Child Matters agenda, which touches all leaders in schools. One area where there has been much development from this policy is in early years practice. Carol Aubrey (2007) has carried out research into groups of early years leaders from children's centres, foundation units in primary schools, and nursery and day-care provision. Here the context is very specific to younger children, and I have argued that working with younger children is a specific emotion context because their feelings are so spontaneous and close to the surface. It is a different kind of emotional display and, as Ben, the headteacher in my study, suggested, makes a special atmosphere for leaders of younger children to work in as they are more consciously aware of the part emotion plays in schools. As well as this aspect, there is also extended schools and liaison with new groups in social care outside the usual boundaries of the school's emotional context.

In terms of emotion and leadership, and some of the arguments I have been making in this book, although the context (system wide, early years) is different, most of the important social aspects of emotion remain important. Leaders will still have a pivotal emotional role, although it may differ in the way it is acted out within a specific organisation. The emotional geography of teaching may look different at first glance, but many of the underlying contours are the same.

Understanding emotionology

I have referred to Fineman's work throughout this book, because I find his approach both illuminating and often in tune with my perspective on emotion. He suggests that organisations are best understood as *emotional arenas* (2000), where emotion is performed for particular audiences. For the headteacher, this audience is a particularly wide and diverse one, encompassing staff, pupils and the wider community. He has expanded on this with the idea of '*emotionologies*'. This concept is one that emphasises the importance of the social aspect of emotion that I have been discussing throughout the book. It is the deep, embedded nature of the affective that is not subject to changing discourses in the study of leadership. Fineman advocates:

> a frame-shift in our understanding of emotion – from an ideologically neutral, within-the-individual, experience to one that is firmly shaped by social structures and the norms and values of the organisation. (2007: 1)

So, he argues, the study of emotions raises questions about power, what we value in organisations, how emotion can be oppressive and silence people – in particular in terms of how we look at men's and women's feelings:

> Social valuation produces an *emotionology* – society's 'take' on the way certain emotions have to be directed and expressed … while emotions have biological roots, they are soon overwritten by social and moral discourses (2007: 2).

This idea is a very helpful one for leaders because it puts the organisation and wider society back into the notion that we call leadership. Fineman argues that emotionologies are shaped by organisational practices, those events that give order and meaning. Some of these might be termed managerial and rational (for example, appraisals, team meetings). Connecting back to 'being a headteacher' he also notes that identity is important, 'it is a process of holding and resolving different social-emotional narratives about who we are, who we were, and who we wish to be' (Fineman, 2008: 5). It is such social-emotional narratives that leaders in education have to deal with on a daily basis, and one of the aspects that differentiates schools from some other human service organisations. Relationships in schools are built up over long periods, unlike hospitals. The relationships are challenging due to their ever-changing nature, unlike prisons. All such human service organisations (at the time of writing) work within a high accountability framework, but failure to achieve targets in education is more public, I would argue.

In a school, leadership at all levels will shape organisational practice and headteachers will still have a significant role to play in setting the scene for these practices. As we saw when we looked at the idea of emotional labour and roles, schools have particular patterns of behaviour that are reinforced over time. What is deemed acceptable at any given time, or any particular school is driven by the emotional context. In a time of change, refinement and innovation in educational leadership, emotion, as noted above, cannot be ideologically neutral. This stance has particular consequences for the headteacher, and links to the sustainability of headship.

How does emotion and leadership link to sustainability of headteachers?

So far, I have argued that understanding your own leadership narrative can aid identity formation as a leader, partly because a narrative can resolve some of the tensions in our social and emotional context, and reaffirm our own values and purpose in schools. At the same time, no headteacher is immune either from the emotional context of the school, or the policy context within which the school sits. The emotionology of schools is a particular one, and headteachers, and senior leaders in schools, are expected to express their emotions in a certain way, which will vary due to some of the factors already discussed. Can such a particular emotional role be sustained over long periods? The whole issue of the sustainability of headship has become of great interest to education policy makers over the last five years. In England and Wales, fewer people than in the past are interested in becoming a school principal. For example, one report (Howson, 2005) revealed that applications to secondary headships had fallen by 2.5 per cent since the report of the previous year, and that the level of unfilled posts was high (secondary: 20.2 per cent; primary: 27.9 per cent; special schools: 22.2 per cent). Perhaps this is not surprising, because with multiple (and often conflicting) accountabilities and the increased demands and heightened expectations, the nature of the job has changed substantially, giving rise to a set of expectations and working conditions that are unattractive (Crawford, 2007). Staff and headteachers may find themselves having to straddle the government's external accountability requirements, with a need and/or belief in sharing leadership in school. This relates to their basic values as educators, and will mean tensions in the way headteachers account for emotion in their own leadership narrative.

The National College for School Leadership (NCSL) has looked at various aspects of leadership sustainability, especially for headteachers. The system, as a whole, needs to consider sustainability, succession planning and to ensure the quality and development of schools. Relating this to the needs of individuals is not easy to do. From the system's perspective, there is a supply problem with large numbers of vacancies anticipated over the next few years. From the perspective of individuals, it is important that people are encouraged to want to do the job first and foremost, and that opportunities are provided to allow aspiring school leaders to acquire appropriate knowledge and understanding which will sustain them over time. Emotional support may also have a place.

Sustainability is two pronged. Those going into leadership positions need to have some assurances that as a role it is sustainable over time. Those already in role, for example as headteachers, have to be aware of strategies that will enable them to sustain their work over lengthy time periods, despite all the tensions discussed above. Some researchers have also asked whether there is a time limit to the headship position (Earley and Weindling, 2004), and it may be that the emotional work of leadership requires time limits of some kind in order for leaders to be at their best. Nevertheless, knowledge of emotion and leadership can help headteachers understand more clearly the issues that are involved in sustainability.

Negotiating oneself around the intricacies of people

In the context of looking at the heart of leadership, I have argued that knowledge of emotion is helpful to the leader, despite the complexities that are involved in understanding all the different approaches that exist. For example, the adaptive functions of emotions are part of the biological background, which can repay examination by headteachers, because they can shed insight on their own and others' behaviour that comes from the past. The cognitive functions of emotion are complex with a variety of perspectives that can be employed. Again, headteachers can find exploration of these useful to their practice because they can help explain some of the more complex aspects of people management in schools. This book has concentrated mainly on the social/cultural side of emotion because of the relevance to practice and how people live and work together in groups in schools with certain norms and values. The power of emotion to affect others is often regulated by norms and the context of schooling at any one time. Social interaction, it could be argued, is at the core of life as lived in schools. It has been argued (Shaver et al., 2001: 27) that knowledge of emotion plays an important part in social interactions as such knowledge can be used to predict, control, direct and interpret what is going on in any given situation.

Shaver et al. also note that 'emotions clearly affect people, and many of these effects have profound social consequences' (2001: 171). They suggest emotions can alter thinking and behaviour, focus on certain aspects of the task rather than others, mark social status and influence impression. All of these are aspects of leading schools, and have connections to sustainability in leadership. As O'Connor discovered when investigating the leadership learning experiences of middle leaders in Ireland:

> Their learning involves dealing with interpersonal relationships and dilemmas. A key challenge is acquiring 'people knowledge' (Eraut, 1994), the issue of dealing with colleagues, Senior Management and other adults: *'negotiating oneself around the intricacies of people'* (respondent). (O'Connor, 2008: 91, emphasis in original)

Sustainability in primary headship may be more significantly influenced by these factors than secondary headship due to the inflexibility of size. A real-life example serves to illustrate this. If there is a headteacher and a staff of 10 (teaching and non-teaching) in an urban primary school setting, the emotional context of the school is much more vulnerable to life effects. For example, suppose the head-teacher has family problems, the deputy is having treatment for a life-threatening illness, and the circumstances of the school are challenging, the burden of accountability may fall on the next most experienced person who only has four years' teaching experience. These sorts of life events are common in schools, and in the worst-case scenarios, the difficulties of the school context can exacerbate the health difficulties of staff, leading to a vicious circle. The illustration I have just given could have led to members of staff feeling that the emotional context of the school was not a pleasant one to work in. They felt they were fortunate, however, as one major event, their Ofsted inspection, had happened before all the difficulties, and had been positive. The acting head was not sure he would have managed it well within the emotional circumstances that prevailed two months later.

This emotional context is important, but not seen as a mitigating factor by many of the educational accountability mechanisms. It is also often not taken into account by the players in the emotional context. That is, they do not feel able to admit to difficulties of an emotional nature as they can be seen as a weakness, even though many of the emotional aspects of school life are not within either the control or remit of the headteacher. Most headteachers whose school fails an Ofsted inspection leave their post, even if their leadership is not suggested as a major factor in the school's lack of educational success. Some judge it would be best for the school if they stepped down to allow a fresh start; others are persuaded by the governing body or the local authority that it would be a good idea, and are often moved sideways into other roles. So, although the rhetoric speaks of distributed leadership, the headteacher knows that s/he will be held to account.

Qualifications

This personal judgement aspect could be one of the main reasons why primary headships in England (and other countries) are experiencing a dearth of applications, and have to be advertised several times. It is also interesting to note that in 2008, of the 30,000 teachers who have passed the National Professional Qualification for Headship (NPQH), just over a third have gone on to apply to headship. This is one of the aspects of sustainability that has prompted the National College for School Leadership in England to re-launch the qualification to try to ensure that only those who really want to apply for headship take the course. This can, of course, be interpreted as making entry to headship tougher, a strange idea perhaps when there are such short-ages. Others would argue that it means that only the best leaders will get through, and thus create fewer problems later on.

The power of emotion and leadership is such that, although it is an influential part of school life, as an issue it is threatening to the status quo. Schools involve a huge amount of 'people work', which cannot avoid emotional issues. Mike Cowie and I have suggested that leadership and manage-ment are 'sanitised' concepts in much of the literature on headship even though the work of headteachers involves working with people (Cowie and Crawford, 2007). People will bring with them unexpected emotional agendas. We noted, as part of a larger study on headteacher preparation, that new heads are surprised by the tensions that arise between the day-to-day 'busy ness' of a school leader, their strategic role, and deeper emotional issues. A study in Scotland by Draper and McMichael found a mismatch between the role expectations of new headteachers and their post-appointment experiences, and that many new heads were ill prepared for the 'bumpy ride of reality' (Draper and

McMichael, 1998: 199). These new headteachers found it useful to have others in a similar situation to network with, and it was one of the most vital aspects of a headship qualification for them – that they were in touch with others.

Past and future

The emotional context is crucial for sustainability, particularly in primary schools. Life events amongst parents and children are closer to staff, and the staff's life events are closer to parents and children than in most secondary schools. There is far less margin for barriers between those in leadership positions and what happens to people emotionally. As one secondary headteacher put it, 'I never realised until I came to this current [small] secondary school, the lack of flexibility and strain that some of my primary colleagues must have every day.' Schools place huge, often unacknowledged demands on their headteachers, and it could be that a growing realisation of this means that fewer people (who have seen the effects at first-hand) are willing to put themselves in such a vulnerable position.

Educational leadership theory is beginning to acknowledge some of these emotional aspects as they relate to sustainability, suggesting that the rational view is not the only explanatory framework for leadership. School leaders have their own emotional needs that are currently not being met. With the current shortage of leaders it is probably not enough to ask, 'How do leaders create a climate in which emotions can be safely discharged without fear of escalation, humiliation or abandonment?' (Harris, 2007: 172) – although this is a question that should be discussed. There is a pressing need to go further and ask how our educational accountability framework can create a climate for the headteachers in primary and secondary schools where they too are able to give the best they have to offer. Some would perhaps argue that it is a moral imperative to do so for the future of education.

Recently, I edited a collection of articles about Alec Clegg, who was the Chief Education Officer of the West Riding of Yorkshire in the post-war period – a time when policy makers flocked to Yorkshire to see fantastic work in schools. One of the reasons that the West Riding was so important a place for dynamic but supported educational change is that Clegg was able to create such an emotional climate. As his Deputy, Peter Newsam, has written:

> Schools cannot directly change society, but they can change children, for the better or for the worse. It follows that, as school teaches how to live as well as the skills to live by, there is a moral duty on all who work in or for schools to ensure that both sorts of lessons are well and truly learned. Within that moral dimension there was a deeply felt compassion. *Children in Distress* written by Clegg with Barbara Megson, was not written by someone whose experience had deluded him into believing that all families are happy. Indeed, his own early school experience, before he decided to start working hard at the age of thirteen, had taught him what failure feels like. After a bad day at school, he would visit his aunt, Mrs Daniel. Telling the story nearly fifty years later, Alec Clegg would throw open his arms and with a broad smile declare, 'And Mrs Daniel would tell me I was *marvellous*'. With that reassurance of long ago in mind, perhaps, Alec Clegg was quick to recognise and respond to a sense of failure in others. 'Don't hesitate to come and see me if you are miserable about anything', he told the assembled advisers at Woolley Hall in 1965. (Newsam, 2008)

Compassion and sustainability are inextricably linked. The humanity of leaders in schools shows even in the small number of leadership narratives in this book. If part of the role of headteacher is to create and sustain an emotional climate for learning in the school, more attention will have to be paid to how they, in turn, are nurtured and encouraged, as well as monitored and evaluated.

> **Think points**
>
> 1 Describe the emotional context of your school. What are the key things that help/hinder sustainability in leadership?
> 2 What could be done to sustain headteachers long term in schools?
> 3 Note down any innovative leadership practices that you are working with or are aware of, such as federations, job share etc. What are the emotional implications for such leadership practices?

Further reading

Aubrey, C. (2007) *Leading and Managing Early Years Settings*. London: Sage.
If you are particularly interested in early years settings, this book is one that you should read in light of the discussions in this chapter of emotion and working with younger children.

Glatter, R. (2006) 'Leadership and organization in education: time for a re-orientation?', *School Leadership and Management*, 26 (1): 69–84.
I have argued that emotional context in the organisation is important. This article suggests that we concentrate too much on leadership to the detriment of organisational issues especially in human service organisations.

Hopkins, D. (2007) *Every School a Great School: Realising the Potential of System Leadership*. Maidenhead: Open University Press.
For further details on system leadership, this book outlines the educational philosophy behind the idea.

Chapter 9

Personal and practical wisdom

The real voyage of discovery consists not in seeking new landscapes, but having new eyes.
(Marcel Proust, French novelist, 1871–1922)

Introduction

This chapter concludes the book by bringing together many of the ideas that have been discussed so far, in order that you can relate them to yourself, your current context, and your own leadership narrative. It discusses the idea of practical wisdom, and how educational leaders can use this as a way of making the task of leadership more do-able, not just for themselves, but for the people they work with. Getting to the heart of leadership is an ongoing emotional task, and this chapter suggests ways of moving understanding on within the leadership field in education.

Getting to the heart

This book has suggested that there are many aspects of feeling and emotion to bear in mind if you wish to get to the heart of leadership. Most of all, in schools emotion is encircled and interpreted through human understandings. Human understanding of emotion is a topic as varied in itself as the more scientific debate on how you define an emotion. Both have a role to play for those who seek to lead others in educational settings. In other words, the biological and psychological aspects of emotion are mediated both by the social setting, and the life history of the people involved. I have taken you on a journey through emotion and educational leadership, in order to investigate emotion and leadership through the stories headteachers tell. This book has given just a few examples of headteachers who wanted to tell their stories. None of them would wish to be seen as exceptional, and none could be classed as failing at the tasks they have set themselves in very different contexts. They told their story for the research I was engaged in at the time, but I hope that there are issues and situations within those stories that will resonate with you. I have suggested that part of the leader's task is to seek to understand more clearly in what ways emotion and leadership are connected. In order to do this I have located headteachers' lives in a more holistic framework, that of the personal leadership narrative. This narrative suggests that emotion, leadership and one's life history are inevitably connected, but more importantly can be used as a tool to engage with the emotional aspects of leadership in a positive manner.

The argument that I have presented is that there should be a closer connection between emotion and leadership in the practice of schools. This connection views emotion as inherent to the practice of leadership rather than separate from it (Crawford and James, 2006). With this view in mind, I hope the discussion begun here sets the scene for more extensive research with larger groups of headteachers, both primary and secondary. Only by carrying out such detailed research will new insights into emotion and leadership in schools be developed.

I have suggested that it is in social relationships, and the stories that are told about such relationships, that the emotions of leadership can be productively examined. Indeed Kemper argues that:

> A very large class of human emotions results from real, anticipated, imagined, or recollected outcomes of social relations. (2004: 46)

The epigraph at the start of this chapter is particularly relevant to this concluding section. In a real sense this book has not sought out new landscapes. It has taken a familiar setting – the school, and its titular head – and looked at it with emotion as the focus. The person of the headteacher, or what I have called their 'emotional being', is a significant part of the social relationships of the school, and pivotal to the way emotions are connected to the organisational quality of leadership in the school (Ogawa and Bossert, 1997). The personal side of headship is part of the overall emotional coherence of the school. Whilst research into emotion has signposted the importance of 'emotion as inherent', much of educational leadership studies have shied away from considering 'leadership as inherent' because this may wrongly suggest trait theories where leaders were seen as 'born not made' (Law and Glover, 2000: 21–2). The twin concepts of 'emotion as inherent' and 'emotion as socially constructed' evoke a perspective on educational leadership that reasserts the importance of the personal side of emotion. At the same time this approach does not sideline as unimportant the social interactions between leaders and followers, or the policy context within which leaders work. Viewing emotion and leadership as important, means that headteachers and leaders in schools have the opportunity to make new interpretations of situations. I have stressed the role of narratives in this process, because I view them as inescapable for research, a point acknowledged by Elliott:

> To acknowledge that what we are writing is a narrative, and not simply a transparent representation of the realities of the research process is also to foreground the role of the imagined audience in shaping the narrative. ... Narratives are a social product whose form is necessarily shaped by the relation of the author to his/her audience. (2005: 165–6)

My narrative, as yours, is woven and told by our values, and what we believe about education, and is often played out with, and through, emotion. Acknowledgement of the power of emotion in schools by leaders is to free up the potential of a clearer, more coherent approach to emotion and educational leadership as one that recognises the power of emotion to sustain and drive educational leadership, and influence learning in schools.

The person of the headteacher

This book has looked at various studies into emotional management, emotional regulation and emotional labour. What all of these have in common is an emphasis on the need for those who interact with the public professionally, such as headteachers, to have a 'professional/rational' part of themselves on display most of the time. This containment and regulation is necessary for the smooth running of schools, and how headteachers present themselves is part of the socialisation of leadership. How they manage the emotions and feelings that occur in everyday interaction were a key part of the stories that headteachers told me. All the headteachers were entirely conscious that there were times when they had to 'act the headteacher' and that often these were the times when they wanted to raise the spirits of others, or alter the mood in a specific setting (for example, Laura sending Christmas cards, and Francesca's comment, 'I put on my eyes and teeth'). Headteachers also noted that extreme feelings could not be managed in such a way (death, serious illness, etc.), and several of them talked about the fact that it was important that others knew when they felt such distress. So, they were able to admit to very difficult feelings, but emotions, such as shame and anxiety, which might reflect on them as a headteacher, were more difficult to handle. They were also aware of the times when they needed to have someone to confide in, either inside or outside the school, but finding that non-judgmental emotional outlet could be difficult at times for them. I have argued that this is one reason for the lack of popularity of the headship role at present.

Gender

Emotional management did not appear at first sight to differ starkly for the male or female headteachers in my research. This may be partially to do with the small sample size, or it may be part of the changing way in which society views men and women in terms of behaviour:

> For two decades, feminism has eroded some of the crudest signs of male patronage and blurred some of the dichotomized 'female' and 'male' emotions. Sportsmen can now cry publicly, as well as whoop for joy (Fineman, 2000: 107).

None of the men in the study reflects the gendered rational/emotional dichotomy, where rationality has been assumed as 'typically masculine' and emotionality as 'typically feminine', and rationality has been judged as the only appropriate behaviour in school leadership. These dichotomies are far too simplistic. It was easier to talk about the task of emotional management with the female headteachers, but this may only reflect my own gender, or their particular personalities.

Personal narratives also reveal some of the complex relationships between gender and emotion in educational leadership. When I started to research emotion and educational leadership, I believed that gender would be of particular importance, but this has not turned out to be the case so far. I think this is due to the overwhelming importance of emotional context in terms of this particular piece of work, and not because gender is not relevant or unimportant to emotion and the headteacher. There is a large and growing amount of work looking at gender and emotion more generally. Psychologists Brody and Hall (2000: 339) suggest that research participants may distort their reports of emotion in ways that conform to gender stereotypes, but I have no evidence that any of the headteachers did this. Stereotypes about women being more emotionally expressive were not seen in this study, and this is probably for several reasons. None of my male headteachers viewed it as the cultural norm to not express emotion. In fact, Ben could be said to be more emotional than several of the women in the sample. Brody and Hall also suggest that men are more emotionally expressive with people they know well, and that both men and women are more comfortable discussing feelings with women (2000: 342). This may have been the case with this exploration of emotion and leadership. They also note that in the majority of studies that look at how accurate people are at decoding non-verbal emotional clues, women score higher across ages, cultures and tasks. The only major difference was with anger, where women were much less accurate than men, especially when the person they were dealing with was male.

'Managing' emotion

For all the headteachers involved in the research, emotion and its management in day-to-day interactions was never far away. This could be seen not only in the stories which I have presented in this book, but also in the way emotional events happened whilst I was in schools researching, for example, Ben and the difficult parent, James 'acting cross'. Emotional management is important to their leadership practice because headteachers often act as a conduit for others' emotions, a trend which is noted in much emotion and leadership research (Beatty, 2002; James, 2003). This management of feelings and the emotional display is particularly pertinent to primary schools because in the context of young children in primary schools, emotional expression is never too far away and it is a natural part of work with younger children.

I have also argued that people differ in terms of their personality which means that some headteachers are much more comfortable with the subject of emotion, and discussing it, than others. Laura was an example of a headteacher who was disarmingly open about emotion and leadership, whilst being very confident as an experienced head in her leadership role. She did not feel in any way challenged or threatened by revealing the emotional side of leadership at her school. Although narrative can provide a safe space, such a tool might serve to reinforce prejudices about the 'soft' nature of emotion and its study if not used rigorously.

Emotional management can have a negative effect on leadership practice. Both men and women have been constrained by the educational leadership literature's focus on rationality to the detriment of understandings and expressions of emotion as important for effective leadership. This may be particularly true in the area of decision-making, which is a vital one for leaders, and why I suggested it as an important emotional texture. George (2000) argues strongly from work carried out in neurology, that the evidence suggests that feelings are necessary to make good decisions, and whilst very intense emotions may make decision-making more difficult, an intense reduction in emotion may also lead to irrational behaviour. Emotional management should not lead to total sublimation of feelings, as this may lead to greater stress. Although there are no particular examples of this in the stories in this book, relevant work on stress (Cooper, Dewe and O'Driscoll, 2001) suggests that this may be the case, and would be an interesting, though challenging, area to research further.

Groups and emotional display

The emotion of revealing feelings through emotional display to others in a group is very little emphasised in educational leadership texts. Yet, as Hess and Kirouac note:

> Such emotion displays provide information not only about the feeling state of the senders, but also about their perception of the world, as well as their relationship with current interaction partners. For example, an anger display informs us that the sender feels wronged in some way and assesses this wrong as one that can be redressed. In addition, an anger display signals dominance and can be considered informative regarding the relative power of the anger expressing individual. (2004: 368)

So, although the heads that I interviewed acknowledged that displays of emotions should be managed, they also saw the power of displays of emotion, whether real or put on for the benefit of the other party. Several of the critical incidents told to me in the original research, but not all in this book (for example, Eleanor and the caretaker, p. 90, David and the constant fight for resources, Mary and the incompetent supply teacher, p. 27) told of this kind of emotional management. They also agreed that they did not ever want to be seen as out of control emotionally, but wanted to discuss ways in which they could flag up emotions such as anger to others in the school (Mary and the incompetent teacher is a good example of this). When emotional management is this conscious, it is part of the head-teacher's day-to-day leadership practice. It may rely for its very effectiveness on the fact that it *is* managed. When headteachers are no longer able to manage and regulate feelings, perhaps because their self is compromised, then stress and ultimately breakdown are the more likely to occur.

Lewis (2004) argues that there are some emotions that are managed more self-consciously than others. Shame and guilt are particularly self-conscious emotions, because only the individual who feels the shame can identify the events that cause them. Lewis notes that all such self-conscious emotions have at their centre the notion of self (2004: 623), which has been stressed throughout this book. Emotion and feeling cannot be separated from the personal history of the headteacher.

Emotional coherence

Personal histories are important. There are links between the headteacher as adult and headteacher as child, especially in terms of behaviours and values. Educational leaders who ignore their own and others' histories will not be able to understand the emotional context of the workplace. In particular, I was surprised by the power of story and the social context to move my respondents, and, in particular, their memories of childhood. Earlier, I noted that an important part of self is the idea of 'place identity' (Hargie and Dickson, 2004). Place identity and its notions of physical, social and autobiographical insideness can be strongly linked to the school setting because it is part of everyone's childhood and many schools are small enough for personal territory and connectedness to others to be very relevant. Ben, for example was very much part of Pennington, in terms of physical and social insideness. The autobiographical side of place identity, knowing 'where you come from', and 'who you are', is clearly drawn out in the life stories of all the headteachers, not just the ones we have learnt more about in this book. Overall, I am suggesting that the educational leadership and emotion literature downgrades the importance of identity, self and emotion. There are strong arguments for more work into the connections between leadership, emotion and the headteacher's life story, as part of the understandings generated from the emotional perspective on leadership. This emotional coherence of leadership may well be necessary, I have suggested, for sustainability of leadership over the long term.

Temperament and identity may also play a part in emotion that is not readily acknowledged in educational leadership studies. Research indicates that the adult and the child are closer together emotionally than we would acknowledge (Caspi, Elder and Bern, 1987; 1988). They argue that there are patterns of childhood emotionality that people carry with them into adulthood. Thirty years after they recorded children, who had been ill-tempered at age eight, they followed up the adults. They discovered that some patterns were relatively enduring over time, if gendered. There are some fascinating examples of the different societal outcomes of ill temper for men and women in the studies. For example, men who were assessed as ill-tempered as children were less likely to stay on at school, and more likely to move jobs. Women who were assessed as ill-tempered were more affected in their home life, having more frequent divorces than women who were assessed as even-tempered at age eight. Further work would be necessary to make more generalisable connections with leaders in education, of course, but such research is relevant. It might even mean asking whether there is a particular temperament that is more or less suitable for headteachers, and if so, what this means for headteacher training and development. This is true especially in the light of theoretical dilemmas within developmental psychology, such as whether emotional development is most influenced by temperament or context (the nature versus nurture debate), or a mixture of both. Saarni, a developmental psychologist, may provide some guidance to leaders when she differentiates between temperament and the social environments that people live and work in:

> Temperament provides some degree of response style consistency over time and across situations, whereas specific emotional reactions yield the variability that comes from the influence of specific contexts, specific appraisals, specific social transactions, and the unique meaning systems that are applied to make sense of emotional experience. (2000: 312)

This concurs with Fineman's recommendation that, 'Ideally, we require theory that collapses the individual/organizational/social distinctions from the outset and builds explanations interrelationally' (Fineman, 2000: 4). This is particularly difficult to achieve in an educational policy context that relies on the rational approach. More manageable perhaps is theory that has certain main assumptions. Although Saarni's work is with children, it is particularly pertinent for discussing the role of personal histories in the way that headteachers view emotion, feeling, and leadership. Our assumptions about the world also permeate any understanding of identity, and the way it interrelates to other social experiences. The assumption that guides Saarni's work on emotional development in children is that 'our emotional experiences are inseparable from our relationships with others' (2000: 319).

Such emotional coherence was a feature of the autobiographical interviews. For example, most of the headteachers in my research talked about a passion for changing and influencing what went on in their schools as a key reason for being a headteacher rather than staying as a classroom teacher or middle manager. This was particularly true of James and Laura in the primary group. Both were experienced heads and could, to some extent, be seen to be deriving their identity as a headteacher from the way that others responded to their skilfully projected images (drawn from experience) of what a headteacher should be. Culture and context are the setting for the individual personal history. If emotions have a function for fulfilling interpersonal and intrapersonal goals, then the headteacher's life so far and how one assumes the identity of headteacher are very important interrelationships for study.

Personal Narratives

I have suggested that the professional and personal identities of the headteacher are linked together in the personal leadership narrative, which frames their practice whether they are aware of this narrative or not. A personal leadership narrative is holistic because it takes in the whole person. The way that a headteacher conceptualises his or her leadership will have an impact on the way that that leadership is then practised. The personal leadership narrative is related to the idea of emotions being both inherent *and* socially constructed. The telling of this narrative can pinpoint aspects of both emotion and feeling, and in this respect can be seen to be related to the Johari window, which allows the reflective learner to combine self examination with feedback from others in order to increase knowledge of the 'unknown self.'

Other studies have also taken an approach that acknowledges headteachers as people. Hall studied six women primary and secondary headteachers, and traced their path to headship. She found that:

parental influences (particularly fathers) were significant influences on the women heads' early independence, self-sufficiency and desire to succeed ... although family of origin is by no means an exclusive influence on future values and behaviour, it shapes perception of which resources achieve which results. (1996: 43–4).

Brody and Hall also focus on the idea of temperament, as they suggest that temperament contributes to gender differences because of early experiences with parents and peers. Reading their thoughts on socialisation links back strongly for me to the personal leadership narrative:

The socialisation of emotional expression is especially influenced by characteristics of the family system, including the parents' own behaviours, their gender role attitudes and behaviours, the quality of their marital relationships, their cultural and social economic backgrounds and the particular gender constellation of the children in their families. For example, the extent to which fathers are involved in childcare has been found to relate to the emotions expressed by their daughters and sons, with involved fathers having sons who express more vulnerability and daughters who express less fear and sadness and more competition relative to their same sex peers. (Brody and Hall, 2000: 345)

In the heads' stories, some examples of this are Francesca identifying with her grandfather ('the only sensible woman in the family), Ben and his parents' active involvement in fostering young children (male role model), Laura as an only child until her brother was born, Eleanor having no siblings, and James's particular gender constellation of being the only boy in the family group. It is important to note that I am not suggesting immediate generalisability from this. Rather, I am pointing towards a very fertile field for further investigation in terms of gender and educational leadership, which acknowledges the importance of the personal leadership narrative. As Brody and Hall point out, 'emotional expression and gender have complex interaction – biological, social and cultural roots' (2000: 347). Continued research to look at how this interaction takes place in the field of educational leadership would be a very useful addition to the work on gender already undertaken in the field.

Emotionally intelligent headteachers

One of the tasks I set myself in this book was to set out some of the riches that were unexplored in different approaches to emotion, and have used the ideas of inherent and social to highlight this. This shows that the present understandings of emotion in the leadership field are at best partial, and at worst a simplification of the most oft-quoted research – emotional intelligence. I want to return briefly to this because the popularity of EI has helped provide the intellectual space to discuss emotion and leadership.

Emotion has become a management commodity. Fineman (2000) argues that it has always been known that certain work relationships require emotional skills (2000: 102), but with EI, what Goleman has succeeded in doing is linking such competences explicitly to business success. Fineman suggests that such management ideas become popular because of 'psychological, cultural and rhetorical factors' (ibid.: 103). If EI might just give a business a competitive edge, then it is something that business leaders should take note of. This is true in education, as in business. As Fineman notes:

> Presenting emotional intelligence as a learned competence or set of competences is a key ingredient of the sell … emotional intelligence is stripped of any 'irrational', 'feminine', even 'feeling' connotations that could worry

> or alienate managers. It is less a celebration of feeling than a resource to enhance managers' 'intelligent', rational control. (2000: 105)

Leading any school is a role that requires emotional skill, and some schools require more of such skills than others. So the climate has been right for EI to take its place amongst other leadership strategies for headteachers. This relates to the cultural factors suggested by Fineman. As headship becomes more difficult to sustain wider, social trends, such as a willingness to discuss stress in organisations, means that EI has been seen as part of a possible solution to a problem of recruitment and sustainability, without addressing some of the deeper issues. It is sobering, however, to bear in mind that success is not so easily defined. As Fineman graphically describes it:

> The search for key, universal, characteristics of managerial success has a long history of futility. If emotionally intelligent managers succeed, so do/have managers who seem to make no conscious choice about how to express their emotions – be they typically kind, charismatic, impassive, volatile, aggressive, autocratic, even ruthless. On this basis it would, at times, be emotionally intelligent to be uncompromising, inflexible, angry or pessimistic. (2000: 109)

In the psychological literature, assessment of the claims of EI has been carried out by Matthews, Zeidner and Roberts (2002), who note that much of Goleman's work demonstrates nothing much new in terms of psychological research as a great deal is already known about emotions and personality. They argue that Goleman makes strong claims 'with little (or scant) empirical backing' (2002: 13). The usefulness and plausibility of EI is due, at least partially I believe, to the fact that it reminds leaders what they probably already knew; that emotion and thinking do work together, and that there has perhaps been too much emphasis on the rational and not enough on the power of emotion and feeling. EI's popularity could also be because rational discussion of emotional competences is emotionally safe, and does not require or suggest a change in internal personal feelings. Headteachers will address the perceived danger of acknowledging and discussing difficult feelings in different ways, and EI may be an approach that is less difficult for many. These are ways that they know are socially acceptable and have been learnt over time. The very parts of the headteacher's own personal leadership narrative that need challenging and changing, if schools are to address some of the deeper parts of leadership sustainability, may not be addressed through a more competency-based approach.

Towards personal and practical wisdom

The idea that educational leadership is inseparable from and influenced by emotion in all its many facets is a persuasive one, yet the current research base is incomplete. In taking you through this book, I have aimed to be holistic in my approach to educational leadership and emotion, linking the discussion to the person and their values. Headteachers should be viewed as emotional beings, with the personal, affective side of their lives brought into more prominence through the utilisation of such development strategies as their personal leadership narrative, as well as other opportunities such as coaching and mentoring. Loader in his personal reflections on emotion and educational leadership argues for a more personal, inherently emotional approach to the role of the principal:

> Leadership has its highs and lows, its successes and failures. Principals cry, laugh, dream and become suspicious. There are times when principals do want the fairy godmother to come and save them. (1997: 3)

Ogawa and Bossert conceptualise leadership as flowing 'through the network of roles that comprise organisations' (1997: 19). If leadership is an organisational quality, then so is emotion. To paraphrase Ogawa and Bossert, it flows through the network of people who comprise schools, but at the same time, emotion in educational leadership resides not only in the organisation, but also in the person of the headteacher; the inherent and socially constructed aspects of emotion working together. Both of these make up the emotional context of the school.

I have also speculated that most headteachers have to perform a delicate emotional balancing act much of the time. They have to build a climate of genuine emotion where acceptance and trust are key, and others not only want to follow them as leaders, but feel able to become leaders themselves. Positive emotional context then becomes a necessary condition of distributed leadership. Heads need to be able to engage themselves and others in the task of emotionalising organisations (Fineman, 2000: 278). Emotionalising schools means that a headteacher allows new understandings of emotion to inform leadership, and to begin to ask how and why emotions shape these processes. All the richness of the research into emotion from many fields of study can add more to educational leadership than a concentration on any one particular perspective.

It is difficult to explain what emotion adds to educational leadership without turning both to descriptions of leadership as an art, and a more philosophical approach. DePree, in his best-selling book on how to succeed at leadership, sums up this viewpoint when he states:

> Leadership is much more an art, a belief, a condition of the heart, than a set of things to do. The visible signs of artful leadership are expressed ultimately, in its practice. (1989: 148)

Emotional ways of knowing about what educational leadership is, allow for the practical, and they allow for deeper meanings as well. Another approach to emotion and leadership would be a philosophical one. It was Aristotle's suggestion that a man (and, of course, woman) of practical wisdom should be able to deliberate well about the things that are good and helpful. Practical wisdom enhances leaders' ability to see that there is a need for change in the way leadership and emotion are viewed.

To put it another way, we should acknowledge leadership to have an emotional side, and be clear about the importance of researching it, because such knowledge is of practical value to headteachers. It links with narrative and emotion coherence because:

> Explicitly asking what values we have implicitly lived our lives by, and holding these up for investigation, can produce profound changes in our understanding of the kind of person we are, what we think of the kind of person we are, and how we live our lives. (Arnaud and LeBon, 2000: 8)

This sort of discussion is also useful because it reminds us that getting to the heart of leadership is about emotion, in the ways that I have suggested in this book. It is also about ideas that connect with emotion such as dispositions, virtues and qualities of character. These also have to be understood by educational leaders if they are to understand both the cognitive and affective parts of leadership. Aristotle says that a man of practical wisdom must be able to deliberate well about the things that are good for him. Emotional development needs to be connected to a broader and deeper reflection on educational leadership by those in schools (McLaughlin, 2005).

Life-enhancing leadership

Getting to the heart of leadership has been presented as a complex issue, which has many facets. Whitaker (1997) argues that it has been a false start when leadership theorists have tried to see what, in the personality and experience of skilled leaders, explains their skills and abilities. He suggests that a more productive avenue is to ask, 'What is it that enables successful organisations to succeed and thrive?' and that this will lead to an answer that is more complex than simply good leadership from the top (1997: 127). Whitaker proposes 'life-enhancing leadership' which helps people to be as effective as they both want to be, and have the potential to be' (ibid.: 128). My argument is that schools succeed and thrive more easily if specific attention is paid to understanding emotion and leadership. By asking what enables successful organisations to succeed and thrive, one of the answers may be that the emotional narrative of the headteacher will influence that context so others can be effective in the jobs that they carry out. Whitaker implicitly acknowledges this when he notes that:

> It is through the countless interpersonal transactions of the school day that people's lives are changed, organisational improvements are made, dreams are realised and needs are met. We need more understanding of those snatched moments in corridors. … Life-centred leadership is essentially a catalytic process, helping others to bring about changes in themselves. (1997: 140)

The headteachers in this book all emphasised the interpersonal nature of headship in terms of getting things done. James, in particular, as the most experienced head, underlined the 'countless interpersonal transactions of the school day' when he talked about how his relatively new inexperienced staff were developing:

> I've got a newer staff coming in which means that a new culture of working together and openness is beginning to develop. There are still the odd situations where unnecessary problems happen and I ask the staff to ask themselves 'Are we working together?' I still think they could be more open emotionally among one another – I mean, a teacher had gone in for an operation, and the staff didn't know, so I was wondering whether I should have told them. It is a fundamental lack of closeness it makes me wonder sometimes – am I doing this wrongly? I've been trying to get them involved, as I don't have the best answer for this school, and maybe some of these things I care too much about!

James defined emotional closeness in terms of knowledge within a small staff group, because he equated care for the children with care for each other as people, not just as teachers. This is what his leadership narrative had taught him about successful primary schools. Larger groups, or leaders with a different leadership narrative might not share this view of closeness.

Even when emotion is acknowledged as important, there will be some leaders who would find this approach temperamentally difficult, or even dangerous in terms of accountability. In a review of headship, Southworth argued that the literature on primary headship, in particular, is far too preoccupied with seeing leadership through the lens of the headteacher, and casting heads as 'pivotal, proprietorial and powerful', whilst in fact the landscape is changing towards distributed and 'learning centred leadership' (2004: 22). The rhetoric of the landscape has indeed changed, but I would argue that the headteacher is still an emotional pivot, even though they may be less proprietorial. Their own emotional well-being is still vital to create the conditions in which other sorts of leadership can develop and thrive. All the heads that I interviewed saw themselves in this pivotal position emotionally, and their personal leadership narrative emphasised their desire to make a difference by being in charge. This does not mean in charge and proprietorial. Laura's answer to what sort of headteacher she was, gives a better clue:

> Somebody who has clear sense of what they are trying to do and has a firm grip on what's happening and what others are doing. I aim to have open lines of communication – so that staff know what I am thinking and why I am thinking it; a spider in the centre of a web, but not an aggressive one!

It is this centrality of the leader emotionally – putting themselves at the heart of leadership in a school – that is seen in the narratives, especially the primary school ones. The headteacher is not dominating and powerful in a masculine, powerful sense, but rather the headteacher's web is the one that he/she spins from his/her own emotional base, and that of the staff, forming an emotional context within which the narrative of education is carried out. To put it another way, more simply, they are able to visualise how they want others to relate to each other within the school (staff, parents and children), and know how to build an emotional coherent context. Hall also notes this in her study (1996). She suggests that the primary headteacher's effectiveness 'depended on her sense of self-efficacy combined with support from others which allowed her to be herself' (1996: 186). She also wondered whether men as managers are as concerned to know and manage self as women, and notes that more research is needed 'into the relationship between men's self-concept and their educational leadership practice (ibid.: 187). The men in my research were concerned to know and manage themselves, and Ben, in particular, was concerned with what it meant to be 'authentic' as a person and headteacher.

Headship has in many ways changed dramatically since Southworth's study in the 1980s and Hall's in the 1990s. At the same time society, as noted at several points within the book, is more culturally attuned to matters of emotion.

Public expression of emotion is more acceptable now than it has been in the past. Hall suggests that her women had a 'concern to communicate and share their vision in a way that they became the staff's' (1996: 199) and were more comfortable with collegial processes than men. As Hall notes, the problem with comparing any study is 'in knowing whether the differences are attributable to gender, the context, or personalities, since both studies involved only a few heads' (ibid.: 201). This study also involves only a few heads, but it differs in the way it was framed to specifically discuss emotion and leadership. In that task, both the male and female heads were able to consciously reflect on aspects of their lives, which were not necessarily part of their daily management tasks. In getting to the heart of leadership there are many of Hall's concerns with control, power and the need to deepen self-knowledge of one's self as a leader.

Conclusion

For educational leaders and future research

In any life journey, the affective plays a major role in tandem with the cognitive experience of the world. Getting to the heart of education leadership requires headteachers to explicitly reflect on their leadership and emotion. This book has:

- emphasised the value of examining the role of headship through an emotional lens, and getting to the heart of education leadership by seeing how emotion interrelates with leadership throughout the organisation
- emphasised the importance of knowing more about literature on emotion outside the leadership field
- aimed to give a voice to the personal in headship through the leadership narrative

- raised questions about the way headship is shaped by personal emotional experience
- signposted the links between life history, relationships at home and work, and socialisation, and given you further literature to explore
- emphasised the idea of emotional coherence to help educational leaders to understand how their own personal emotional coherence is related to others in the organisation
- emphasised how a healthy emotional context allows schools to progress more effectively, and with less emotional labour for the headteacher.

This book has been reflective from the beginning. These conclusions cannot be seen as the final answer, but rather the beginning of a conceptualisation of emotion and leadership that moves the discussion beyond the current conceptualisation in education leadership studies. Such a conceptualisation does not treat feelings and emotions as 'objects' that are separate from organisational practice. Rather it suggests that they are inherent to it. It also moves the thinking away from a somewhat restricted view of feelings and emotions in the educational literature, which often limits them to conscious experience (EI) and suggests looking more widely at research into emotion.

Robinson (2001) notes that leadership occurs 'when ideas expressed in talk or action are recognised by others as capable of progressing tasks or problems that are important to them' (2001: 93). It is through this personal emotional coherence that important things happen, and in schools, whether in federations or on their own, it is often the headteacher who not only drives forward these ideas, but takes them to a wider audience. The headteachers I have talked about in this book would probably not stand out in a crowd of headteachers, but all were carrying out their respective roles carefully and effectively. What made them stand out for me was the depth of their emotional commitment to both people (staff, children, parents) and education more generally. Senge tells us that:

> Most of the outstanding leaders I have worked with are neither tall nor especially handsome; they are often mediocre public speakers; they do not stand out in a crowd and they do not mesmerise an attending audience with their brilliance or eloquence. Rather, what distinguishes them is the clarity and persuasiveness of their ideas, the depth of their commitment and their openness to continually learning more. They do not have 'the answer'. But they do instil confidence in those around them that together 'we can learn whatever we need to learn in order to achieve the results we truly desire'. The ability of such people to be natural leaders, as near as I can tell, is the *by-product of a lifetime of effort* to develop conceptual and communication skills, to reflect on personal values and to align personal behaviour with values, to learn how to listen and to appreciate others and others' ideas. (1990: 359, emphasis in original)

In the face of more and more pressure, headteachers' skills in my research were 'the by-product of a lifetime of effort', and were developed as they engaged with their personal leadership narrative. Their reflections on emotion and leadership have enabled me to reconceptualise some of the ideas that I initially had about what being a headteacher means in schools today. They were not only emotionally committed, but also emotionally coherent in their work in schools.

The research I have carried out so far into emotion and leadership has shown that there is still only a partial understanding of both 'emotion and leadership', and how this relates to headship. If I were to do this study again, I would spend longer on the life history of the headteachers. This is because I have seen that through discussions of life history much more can be learnt about emotion and educational leadership than I at first envisaged, especially in terms of personal professional development. Drawing on life history can have many benefits, including:

- Benefits from engaging in self-reflection, both in terms of self-knowledge and a quiet space to reflect.
- Making theory more meaningful and accessible, and providing an important link between research and practice.
- Being therapeutic at difficult times in headship. (Goodson and Sikes, 2001: 73–4).

With such an approach each facet of the personal leadership narrative could be broken down and examined more closely. The concept of a personal leadership narrative could then be developed and adjusted further. More sustained work could also be carried out on collecting the life histories, for example, of both the staff and the headteacher in a primary school. This could help researchers to look more closely at how the emotional context of the organisation is sustained.

For you as an educational leader

To finish, I want to leave you with some final thoughts and some caveats. Researchers into personality suggest that people will agree most with theories that reflect how we see ourselves in the first place (Haviland-Jones and Kahlbaugh, 2004).This may well be so in the case of this book, though I have tried to mitigate this effect. Nevertheless, it was a privilege to share part of these headteachers' stories about themselves, their emotions and their schools. This chapter has spoken, albeit briefly, of philosophy and the idea of practical wisdom. In a sense, the arguments put forward here are philosophical because:

> Philosophers rarely settle or resolve philosophical questions, and unsettability or irresolvability are perhaps hallmarks of a philosophical question. Philosophical debate – and disagreement – goes on. (McLaughlin, 2005: 3)

At a time of recruitment difficulties, there is an urgent need to develop understandings of emotion and school leadership specifically by carrying out further research into the area. Various understandings from the different perspectives on emotion could be developed for headteachers and at all levels of leadership, so that it is not only EI that receives prominence in discussions that feature the affective side of life in a school. Shared understandings of leadership and emotion will be even more necessary in a developing policy context of changes to the ways schools are led. There are many questions that need to be asked for policy development. For example, will 'executive' headship of primary schools promote emotional coherence? And if so, how?

To paraphrase Southworth (1995: 3), what I offer here is neither a definitive set of insights into emotion and leadership, a handbook of development activities, nor a model of how to conduct research into educational leadership and emotion. There is much more to study and to learn about this difficult and demanding topic. The difficulties that can arise when emotion and educational leadership is discussed should not be a barrier, but act as a spur for greater endeavour. Emotional coherence both sustains leadership and helps leaders interpret context more effectively.

Educational leadership cannot, and does not, function without emotion. Emotionally coherent headship is both an emotional quality of the headteachers and at the same time a quality of the social relationships of the school. Over the next few years as there are even more changes in the nature of educational leadership, and as the Every Child Matters (ECM) agenda is fully implemented, this emphasis on the personal and social relations is even more crucial. To sum up, educational leadership is about people, and people necessarily work in an emotional context. I hope that educational leaders will see the value of a deeper conceptualisation of emotion and leadership that moves the discussion beyond the current focus in education leadership studies.

Research into emotion outside of the leadership field is a rich area for discussion, examination and source of 'practical wisdom'. Emotion research has already shaped the educational leadership field, primarily by its emphasis on emotional intelligence, but also through some emphasis on the psychodynamic. Whilst this has had its advantages, I would argue that the educational leadership field has only begun to discover how research into emotion can enrich educational leadership. More emphasis on emotional coherence, perhaps through the stories of headteachers, and the emotional interactions that occur within the school context, could be one way of facilitating this.

And finally

My understanding of emotion and leadership has been enriched by headteachers' stories. Their stories have shaped both their practice and my understanding of it. All stories can be read in different ways, and this book invites you to tell your story in ways that will move you forward as an emotional being in leadership. Telling stories is not, as it would appear, an easy task. It is one that can enrich understanding, and build new knowledge. This is summed up by Wells (1987: 2) who introduces his work on language development in children by justifying his use of storytelling:

> Some readers may be surprised at my use of the word 'story'. But I have chosen it quite deliberately. Stories are a way of making sense – of giving meaning to observable events by making connections between them. However,

for any set of events there is almost always more than one possible interpretation – as a day in any courtroom would amply demonstrate. Carrying out research is, in this respect, like any other form of enquiry based on evidence. Only a certain number of events can be observed and although, like good detectives, researchers have hunches to guide them in choosing what events to observe and what clues to look for, in the last resort they have to go beyond the evidence in order to present a coherent account. The available evidence is given meaning by being embedded in a story in which it makes sense.

Stories, like other language forms, are created in the telling. They are influenced of course, by other stories … They also have history in the accumulated experience of the storyteller. But, most important, a story is the expression of the present attempt by the teller to find meaning in those experiences. My purpose in writing this book, therefore, is to make sense of the evidence that was collected during the research project and of the ideas that I have obtained through reading and discussion, and to tell the meaning that I have made to others who share my concerns. Seen from this perspective, there can be no true stories. The evidence is never so complete or unambiguous as to rule out alternative interpretations. The important criteria in judging the work of a story are: does it fit the facts as I have observed them and does it provide a helpful basis for future action?

This book, as both the story of an individual's journey through research into emotion, and also the stories of individual headteachers, hopes to have fulfilled those important criteria.

References

Ackerman, R. and Maslin-Ostrowski, P. (2004) 'The wounded leader and emotional learning in the schoolhouse', *School Leadership and Management*, 24 (3): 311–28.

Argyris, C. (1996) *Organizational Learning*. Reading, MA: AddisonWesley.

Argyris, C. (1999) *On Organisational Learning*. Oxford: Blackwell.

Arnaud, D. and LeBon, T. (2000) 'Aristotle's distinctions between Theoretical Wisdom, Practical Wisdom and Moral Virtue', *Practical Philosophy*, 3 (1): 6–9.

Ashforth, B. and Tomiuk, M.A. (2000) 'Emotional labour and authenticity: views from service agents', in S. Fineman (ed.) *Emotion in Organizations*. London: Sage.

Aubrey, C. (2007) *Leading and Managing Early Years Settings*. London: Sage.

Barley, S. and Kunda, G. (1992) 'Design and devotion: surges of rational and normative ideologies of control in managerial discourse', *Administrative Science Quarterly*, 37 (3): 363–99.

Beatty, B.R. (2002) 'Emotion matters in educational leadership: examining the unexamined'. Graduate Department of Theory and Policy Studies in Education, Ontario Institute for Studies in Education. Toronto: University of Toronto.

Bennett, N. (1995) *Managing Professional Teachers*. London: Paul Chapman.

Berger, P. and Luckmann, T. (1991) *The Social Construction of Reality*. London: Penguin.

Blackmore, J. (1999) *Troubling Women: Feminism, Leadership and Educational Change*. Maidenhead: Open University Press.

Bottery, M. (2004) *The Challenges of Educational Leadership*. London: Paul Chapman.

Briner, R. (1999) 'The neglect and importance of emotion at work', *European Journal of Work and Organizational Psychology*, 8 (3): 323–46.

Brody, L.R. and Hall, J.A. (2000) 'Gender, emotion and expression', in M. Lewis and J. Haviland-Jones (eds) *Handbook of Emotions*. New York: Guilford Press.

Bush, T. and Glover, D. (2004) *Leadership Development: Evidence and Beliefs*. Lincoln University: National College for School Leadership.

Carlyle, D. and Woods, P. (2002) *Emotions of Teacher Stress*. Stoke-on-Trent: Trentham Books.

Caspi, A., Elder, G.H. and Bern, D. (1987) 'Moving against the world: life course patterns of explosive children', *Developmental Psychology*, 23 (2): 308–13.

Caspi, A., Elder, G.H. and Bern, D. (1988) 'Moving against the world: life course patterns of shy children', *Developmental Psychology*, 24 (6): 824–31.

Coleman, M. (2002) *Women as Headteachers: Striking the Balance*. Stoke-on-Trent: Trentham Books.

Cooper, C.L., Dewe, P.J. and O'Driscoll, M.P. (2001) *Organizational Stress: A Review and Critique of Theory, Research, and Applications*. Thousand Oaks, CA: Sage.

Cortazzi, M. (2002) 'Analysing narratives and documents', in M. Coleman and A.R.J. Briggs (eds) *Research Methods in Educational Leadership and Management*, London: Paul Chapman.

Cowie, M. and Crawford, M. (2007) 'Principal preparation – still an act of faith?', *School Leadership and Management*, 27 (2): 129–46.

Crawford, M. (2002) 'The charismatic school leader – potent myth or persuasive effect?', *School Leadership and Management*, 22 (3): 231–87.

Crawford, M. (2003) 'Challenging circumstances: the role of distributed and intensified leadership', in N. Bennett and L. Anderson (eds) *Rethinking Educational Leadership*. London: Paul Chapman.

Crawford, M. (2004) 'Leadership and emotion in the primary school – reflections from four primary headteachers', *Education 3–13*, 32 (1): 20–25.

Crawford, M. (2007) 'Emotional coherence in primary school headship', *Educational Management Leadership and Administration*, 35 (4): 521–34.

Crawford, M., Edwards, R. and Kydd, L. (eds) (1998) *Taking Issue: Debates in Guidance and Counselling in Learning*. London: Routledge.

Crawford, M. and James, C.R. (2006) 'An affective paradigm for educational leadership practice and research'. University of Warwick: BERA.

Damasio, A. (2004) *Looking for Spinoza: Joy, Sorrow and the Feeling Brain*. London: Vintage.

Denzin, N. (1984) *On Understanding Emotion*. San Francisco: Jossey-Bass.

DePree, M. (1989) *Leadership is an Art*. New York: Dell Publishing.

Derlerga, V. and Berg, J. (eds) (1987) *Self-Disclosure: Theory, Research and Therapy*. New York: Springer.

Dillard, C.B. (1995) 'Leading with her life: an African feminist (re)interpretation of leadership for an urban high school principal', *Educational Administration Quarterly*, 31 (4): 539–63.

Dollard, M.F., Dormann, C., Boyd, C.M., Winefield, H.R. and

Winefield, A.H. (2003) 'Unique aspects of stress in human service work', *Australian Psychologist*, 38 (2): 84–91.

Draper, J. and McMichael, P. (1998) 'Making sense of primary headship: the surprises awaiting new heads', *School Leadership and Management*, 18 (2): 197–211.

Duke, D.D. (1998) 'The normative context of organizational leadership', *Educational Administration Quarterly*, 34 (2): 165–95.

Earley, P. and Weindling, D. (2004) *Understanding School Leadership*. London: Paul Chapman.

Elliott, J. (2005) *Using Narrative in Social Research*. London: Sage.

Epstein, S. (1998) *Constructive Thinking: The Key to Emotional Intelligence*. Westport, CT: Praeger.

Eraut, M. (1994) *Developing Professional Knowledge and Competence*. London: Falmer.

Erikson, E. (1980) *Identity and the Life Cycle*. New York: W.W. Norton.

Fiedler, F. (ed.) (1978) *Situational Control and a Dynamic Theory of Leadership*. Harmondsworth: Penguin.

Fineman, S. (1995) 'Stress, emotions and intervention', in T. Newton (ed.), *Managing Stress: Emotion and Power at Work*. London: Sage.

Fineman, S. (ed.) (2000) *Emotion in Organizations*. London: Sage.

Fineman, S. (2001) 'Emotions and organizational control', in R.L. Payne and L. Cooper (eds) *Emotions at Work*. Chichester: Wiley and Son.

Fineman, S. (2003) *Understanding Emotion at Work*. London: Sage.

Fineman, S. (2005) 'Appreciating emotion at work – paradigm tensions', *International Journal of Work, Organization and Emotion*, 1 (1): 4–19.

Fineman, S. (2008) *The Emotional Organization: Passions and Power*. Oxford: Blackwell.

Frost, P. and Robinson, S. (1999) 'The toxic handler: organizational hero and casualty', *Harvard Business Review*, (July–August): 96–106.

Gabriel, Y. (1999) *Organizations in Depth*. London: Sage.

Gabriel, Y. (2000) *Storytelling in Organizations: Facts, Fiction, and Fantasies*. Oxford: Oxford University Press.

General Teaching Council for England (GTCE) (2006) *Survey of Teachers 2006*. Available online at: www.gtce.org.uk/research

George, J.M. (2000) 'Emotions and leadership: the role of emotional intelligence', *Human Relations*, 53 (8): 1027–55.

Gerrod Parrot, W. (ed.) (2001) *Emotions in Social Psychology*. Hove: Taylor and Francis.

Gerrod Parrott, W. and Spackman, M. (2000) 'Emotion and memory', in M. Lewis and J. Haviland-Jones (eds) *Handbook of Emotions*. New York: Guilford Press.

Ginsberg, R. and Davies, T. (2002) 'The emotional side of leadership', in M. Bennett, M. Crawford and M. Cartwright (eds), *Effective Educational Leadership*. London: Paul Chapman.

Gladwell, M. (2005) *Blink: The Power of Thinking without Thinking*. London: Penguin.

Glatter, R. (2006) 'Leadership and organization in education: time for a re-orientation?', *School Leadership and Management*, 26 (1): 69–84.

Goddard, J.T. (1998) *Of Daffodils and Dog Teams: Reflections on Leadership*. Warwick: British Educational Management and Administration Society (BEMAS).

Goffman, E. (1961) *Encounters: Two studies in the Sociology of Interaction*. New York: Bobbs-Merrill.

Goleman, D. (1995) *Emotional Intelligence*. New York: Bantam.

Goodley, D., Lawthom, R., Clough, P. and Moore, M. (2004) *Researching Life Stories*. London: RoutledgeFalmer.

Goodson, I. and Sikes, P. (2001) *Life History Research in*

Educational Settings: Learning from Lives. Buckingham: Open University Press.

Gronn, P. (2003) *The New Work of New Educational Leaders: Changing Leadership Practice in an Era of School Reform.* London: Paul Chapman.

Gronn, P. and Lacey, K. (2004) 'Positioning oneself for leadership: feelings of vulnerability among aspirant school principals', *School Leadership and Management*, 24 (4): 405–24.

Gronn, P. and Ribbins, P. (1996) 'Leaders in context: post-positivist approaches to understanding educational leadership', *Educational Administration Quarterly*, 32 (3): 452–73.

Gunter, H. (1999) 'Researching and constructing histories of the field of education management', in T. Bush, L. Bell, R. Bolam, R. Glatter and P. Ribbins (eds) *Education Management: Redefining Theory, Policy and Practice.* London: Paul Chapman.

Hall, V. (1996) *Dancing on the Ceiling: A Study of Women Managers in Education.* London: Paul Chapman.

Halpin, D. (2003) *Hope and Education: The Role of the Utopian Imagination.* London: RoutledgeFalmer.

Hargie, O. and Dickson, D. (2004) *Skilled Interpersonal Communication.* London: Routledge.

Hargreaves, A. (1994) *Changing Teachers, Changing Times.* New York: Teachers College Press.

Hargreaves, A. (2000) *Emotional Geographies: Teaching in a Box.* New Orleans: AERA.

Harris, B. (2007) *Supporting the Emotional Work of School Leaders.* London: Paul Chapman.

Hatcher, C. (2008) 'Becoming a successful corporate character and the role of emotional management', in S. Fineman (ed.) *The Emotional Organization: Passion and Power.* Oxford: Blackwell.

Haviland-Jones, J. and Kahlbaugh, P. (2004) 'Emotion and

identity', in M. Lewis and J. Haviland-Jones (eds) *Handbook of Emotions*. New York: Guilford Press.

Hess, U. and Kirouac, G. (2004) 'Emotion expression in groups', in M. Lewis and J. Haviland-Jones (eds) *Handbook of Emotions*. New York: Guilford Press.

Hirschhorn, L. (1997) *The Workplace Within: Psychodynamics of Organizational Life*. Cambridge, MA: MIT Press.

Hochschild, A.R. (1983) *The Managed Heart: Commercialization of Human Feeling*. Berkeley: University of California Press.

Hopkins, D. (2007) *Every School a Great School: Realising the Potential of System Leadership*. Maidenhead: Open University Press.

Howe, D. (1993) *On Being a Client: Understanding the Process of Counselling and Psychotherapy*. London: Sage.

Howson, J. (2005) *Eleventh Annual Report. The State of the Labour Market for Senior Staff in Schools in England and Wales*. Oxford: Education Data Surveys.

James, C. (2000) 'Managing the emotional dimension: the key leadership task in radical educational change'. *BEMAS Research Conference*, Cambridge.

James, C. (2003) 'The work of educational leaders in building creative and passionate schools and colleges'. *BELMAS conference*, Milton Keynes.

James, C.R. and Jones, N. (2003) 'Decision-making in secondary schools: a case study of the effect of emotion on espoused theories, theories in use and resistance to change'. Paper presented at the Annual Conference of the British Educational Leadership, Management and Administration Society, Milton Keynes.

Josselson, R. and Lieblich, A. (eds) (1995) *The Narrative Study of Lives*. London: Sage.

Kemper, T.D. (2004) 'Social models in the explanation of emotions', in M. Lewis and J. Haviland-Jones (eds) *Handbook of Emotions*. New York: Guilford Press.

Law, S. and Glover, D. (2000) *Educational Leadership and Learning*. Buckingham: Open University Press.

Layard, R. (2005) *Happiness: Lessons from a New Science*. London: Penguin.

Leithwood, K., Jantzi, D. and Steinbach, R. (1999) *Changing Leadership for Changing Times*. Buckingham: Open University Press.

Levenson, R.W. (1999) 'The intrapersonal functions of emotion', *Cognition and Emotion*, 13 (5): 481–504.

Lewis, M. (2004) 'Self-conscious emotions: embarrassment, pride, shame and guilt', in M. Lewis and J. Haviland-Jones (eds) *The Handbook of Emotions*. New York: Guilford Press.

Loader, D. (1997) *The Inner Principal*. London: Falmer Press.

Lupton, D. (1998) *The Emotional Self*. London: Sage.

McLaughlin, T. (2005) 'What's wrong with emotional literacy and emotional intelligence?'. University of London: Institute of Education.

Matthews, G., Zeidner, M. and Roberts, R.D. (2002) *Emotional Intelligence: Science and Myth*. Cambridge, MA: MIT Press.

Meyerson, D. and Martin, J. (1997) 'Cultural change: integration of three different views', in A. Harris, N. Bennett and M. Preedy (eds) *Organisational Effectiveness and Improvement in Education*. Buckingham: Open University Press.

Moller, J. (2005) 'Coping with accountability', in C. Sugrue (ed.) *Passionate Principalship: Learning from the Life History of Leaders*. London: RoutledgeFalmer.

Morgan, G. (1998) *Images of Organisations*. Thousand Oaks, CA: Sage.

Murphy, J. and Beck, L.G. (1994) 'Reconstructing the principalship: challenges and possibilities', in J. Murphy and K. Seashore-Lewis (eds) *Reshaping the Principalship: Insights from Transformational Reform Efforts*. Thousand Oaks, CA: Corwin Press.

Newsam, P. (2008) 'What price hyacinths? An appreciation of the work of Sir Alec Clegg', *Education 3–13*, 36 (2): 109–16.

Newton, T., Handy, J. and Fineman, S. (1995) *Managing Stress: Emotion and Power at Work*. London: Sage.

O'Connor, E. (2008) *'There is a lot to be Learnt': Assistant Principals' Perceptions of their Professional Learning Experiences and Learning Needs in their Role as Middle Leaders in Irish Post-Primary Schools*. London: Institute of Education.

Oatley, K. and Jenkins, J.M. (2003) *Understanding Emotions*. Oxford: Blackwell.

Ogawa, R.T. and Bossert, S.T. (1997) 'Leadership as an organisational quality', in M. Crawford, L. Kydd and C. Riches (eds) *Leadership and Teams in Educational Management*. Buckingham: Open University Press.

Pascal, C. and Ribbins, P. (1998) *Understanding Primary Headteachers*. London: Cassell.

Pekrun, R. and Frese, M. (1992) 'Emotions in work and achievement', *International Review of Industrial and Organizational Psychology*, 7: 153–200.

Richardson, E. (1973) *The Teacher, the School and the Task of Management*. London: Heinemann.

Roberts, B. (2002) *Biographical Research*. Buckingham: Open University Press.

Robinson, V. (2001) 'Embedding leadership in task performance', in K. Wong and C.W. Evers (eds), *Leadership for Quality Schooling: International Perspectives*. London: RoutledgeFalmer.

Saarni, C. (2000) 'The social context of emotional development', in M. Lewis and J. Haviland-Jones (eds) *Handbook of Emotions*. New York: Guilford Press.

Sachs, J. and Blackmore, J. (1998) 'You never show you can't cope: women in school leadership roles managing their emotions', *Gender and Education*, 10 (3): 265–80.

Salovey, P. and Mayer, P. (1990) 'Emotional intelligence', *Imagination, Cognition and Personality*, 9: 185–211.

Salovey, P. and Mayer, P. (2001) 'Emotional intelligence', in K. Oatley and J.M. Jenkins (eds) *Human Emotions: A Reader*. Oxford: Blackwell.

Sandelands, L.E. and Boudens, C.J. (2000) 'Feeling at work', in S. Fineman (ed.) *Emotion in Organizations*. London: Sage.

Sarbin, T.R. (1989) 'Emotions as narrative emplotments', in M. Packer and R. Addison (eds) *Entering the Circle: Hermeneutic Investigation in Psychology*. Albany, NY: Suny Press.

Schein, E.H. (1985) *Organisational Culture and Leadership*. San Francisco: Jossey-Bass.

Seidman, I. (1998) *Interviewing as Qualitative Research*. New York: Teachers College Press.

Seligman, M., Park, N. and Peterson, C. (2005) 'Positive psychology progress', *American Psychologist*, 60 (5): 410–21.

Senge, P. (1990) *The Fifth Discipline*. London: Century Business.

Sergiovanni, T. (1995) *The Headteachership: A Reflective Practice Perspective*. Boston: Allyn and Bacon.

Sergiovanni, T.J. (2003) 'The lifeworld at the center: values and action in educational leadership', in N. Bennett, M. Crawford and M. Cartwright (eds) *Effective Educational Leadership*. London: Paul Chapman.

Shaver, P., Schwartz, J., Kirson, D. and O'Connor, C. (2001) 'Emotion knowledge: further exploration of a prototype approach', in W. Gerrod Parrott (ed.) *Emotions in Social Psychology*. Hove: Taylor and Francis.

Shields, C. (2004) 'Dialogic leadership for social justice: overcoming pathologies of silence', *Educational Administration Quarterly*, 40 (1): 109–32.

Singer, J.A. and Salovey, P. (1996) 'Motivated memory: self-defining memories, goals, and affect regulation', in L.

Martin and A. Tesser (eds) *Striving and Feeling: Interactions Among Goals, Affect, and Self-Regulation*. Hillsdale, NJ: Erlbaum.

Southworth, G. (1995) *Looking into Primary Headship: A Research Based Interpretation*. London: Falmer.

Southworth, G. (2004) *Primary School Leadership in Context: Leading Small, Medium and Large Sized Schools*. London: RoutledgeFalmer.

Waldron, V. (2000) 'Relational experiences and emotion at work', in S. Fineman (ed.) *Emotion in Organizations*. London: Sage.

Wells, G. (1987) *The Meaning Makers: Children Learning and Using Language to Learn*. London: Heinemann.

West-Burnham, J. and Ireson, J. (2006) *Leadership Development and Personal Effectiveness*. Nottingham: NCSL.

Whitaker, P. (1997) *Primary Schools and the Future*. Buckingham: Open University Press.

Index